St. Paul: the Apostle & His Letters

Norman Madsen

Our Sunday Visitor Publishing Division
Our Sunday Visitor, Inc.
Huntington, Indiana 46750

International Standard Book Number:
0-87973-589-9

Library of Congress Catalog Card Number:
85-62816

Cover design by James E. McIlrath

Printed in the United States of America

589

For
Alice M. Madsen

Contents

Preface

On almost every occasion of formal Christian worship one encounters a reading from the Apostle Paul's letters. Like the Old Testament, Paul has often been considered a "secondary" source for Christian understanding and enlightenment. The New Testament Gospels have traditionally held primary importance, evidenced by the fact that during formal worship services parishioners stand for the reading of the Gospel.

Yet Paul's writings (and the Old Testament) form an essential part of Christian tradition. It is interesting to note that in the very early Church the scriptural readings were these "secondary" sources, that is, Paul and the Old Testament. Probably following the synagogue order of worship, where the Scriptures were read at each service, the early Christians initially relied upon the Jewish Scriptures, at least until the letters of Paul were written and circulated (between the late A.D. 40s and early 60s). Once the disciples and Apostles began to exit this life for their heavenly home, either through martyrdom or because of natural death, Gospels began to appear as written substitutes of their authority. These writings eventually moved to the forefront of Christian influence, reducing the letters of Paul and the Old Testament to secondary Christian sources.

However, if one were to consider the influence of Paul's letters on the history of Christian thought, the result is quite surprising. St. Augustine, to take but one ex-

1

ample, was converted in the garden when he read a section of Paul's Letter to the Romans. He tells us in his *Confessions*:

> *And behold I heard a voice (whether a boy's voice or a girl's I do not know) from a nearby house, saying melodically and repeating over and over: "Take and read; take and read." Holding back a flood of tears, I arose, interpreting this event as nothing other than a divine command to open my book of scriptures and to read the first passage upon which my eyes would have fallen.*

He then reads Romans 13:13-14: ". . . not in reveling and drunkenness, not in debauchery and licentiousness, not in quarreling and jealousy. But put on the Lord Jesus Christ, and make no provision for the flesh. . . ." From that moment Jesus Christ had a new Apostle and the Church had a new Father.

Quotes from Paul's letters are found throughout the writings of the Church Fathers from the earliest times. This influence carries through to the Reformation when both Luther and Calvin were deeply and profoundly influenced by Paul. In this century, at least one important theologian, Karl Barth, entered the "strange new world of the Bible" by way of Paul's Letter to the Church at Rome and later through a study of Philippians. It follows that Paul's writings are essential not just for the Christian theologian, but for all believers who would understand and live the Christian faith.

Our plan will be to first apprehend Paul the person and his writings. At the outset, we will consider his life. What can we know about this great Apostle? Where did he live at various times in his life and where did he travel? To whom did he write his letters? Why did he write those letters? What was the situation in those congregations he addressed? What were his struggles?

Second, we will attempt to examine his letters. What can we know about Christian believers in first-century Christianity? We will consider the general content of each individual letter before turning to selected key passages from each Epistle. These passages will be chosen for their essential importance to Paul's presentation of the Gospel and because of their enduring and timeless themes. This of course presents a problem, the task of selecting a few "gems" from a huge treasure chest. However the choice is made, there is always the sense of missing key passages. I have attempted to compensate for this by often summarizing sections, realizing that at times even this is insufficient.

Nevertheless, it is hoped that this type of study will produce a sense of the Apostle and his importance for the Christian faith. Either by reading a few pages as a daily devotional, or by reading the entire volume as an introduction to Paul, it is hoped that spiritual stimulation will result by way of some inspiration, some insight, some understanding, some direction. Surely we cannot but gain on our own spiritual journey by considering the greatest interpreter of the Christian faith. He will be our lens for focusing on the essence of Christianity — he will be our saint. What could be said of Paul applies to all Christians.

> *God creates out of* nothing. *Wonderful, you say. Yes, to be sure, but He does what is still more wonderful: He makes saints out of sinners.*
>
> Soren Kierkegaard, *Journals*

I wish to thank all who participated in making this

3

book a reality. Among those I am especially grateful to are Pam Fetters, who read the proofs and offered valuable suggestions, and Pat Moran of Our Sunday Visitor, for his editorial support.

Norman P. Madsen

All Saints Day,
November 1, 1985

4

MAIN EVENTS IN THE LIFE OF PAUL
(All Dates Are Approximate)

Birth	A.D. 10
Death of Christ	30
Conversion of Paul	32
Years in Arabia (?)	32-35
Preaching in Damascus and First Jerusalem Visit	35
Hidden Years (In Tarsus)	35-46
Barnabas Brings Paul to Antioch	46-47
Second Jerusalem Visit	47
First Missionary Journey	47-48
Third Jerusalem Visit	49
(Letter to the Galatians?)	(49?)
Letters to the Thessalonians	50-51
Second Missionary Journey	50-53
(Letter to the Galatians?)	(54-55?)
Letters to the Corinthians	55
Third Missionary Journey	53-57
Letter to the Romans	56
Jerusalem Arrest	57
Trial, Journey to Rome and House Arrest in Rome	57-62
Prison Epistles (Philemon, Colossians[?], Ephesians[?], Philippians	59-62
Martyrdom	62-64
(Travels to Spain and Writing of Pastoral Epistles?)	(65-?)

CHAPTER ONE

Paul as an Apostle of Christ Jesus

• *Paul the Person*

We really can know very little about historical persons. Attempts to capture their *living* personality is only possible through indirect methods, that is, they are knowable through those who knew them or by way of their remaining personalia. The Apostle Paul is no exception. However, we do have both the above mentioned sources at our disposal for studying his character. We have a writing which tells much about his life. Entitled the Acts of the Apostles, it is the first real volume of Church history. Second, and of greater value, we have his own writings which include some personal testimony of his background (Galatians 1:13-2:10 and Philippians 3:5-6).

Paul categorically states that he was primarily a proclaimer of the Good News, or Gospel. This was his calling in life and it dominated his latter years. Theological debate and doctrinal discussions were of secondary importance — valuable only as they supported his proclaimed message. In the end, Paul's writings and proclamations tell of an individual who was sensitive, compassionate, caring; a person who lived and experienced that which was the essence of his life. His vocation stemmed from practical acquaintances gained through repeated trials and varied personal observation, experiences and sufferings. Paul was an intensely *practical* individual who spoke sensitively to others of spiritual truths — and that is the wonder of his timelessness.

This experiential quality in Paul is in a way the true originality of his character. His intense practical experience was motivated by a unique combination of two spiritual forces, his power of debate and the inspiration of the Holy Spirit. Add to this originality traits noted by various scholars, religious writers and thinkers through the years: characteristics such as his heart of fire, imagination, sincerity, tact, courage, womanlike tenderness, genius for organization, his mystical intuitions, his moral keenness and observation, resolute will, logical mind, and we begin to capture a better sense of the person. The blending of these many traits made him the Apostle for the nations, the master builder for both Christian thought and the universal body of Christ, the Church.

Though spiritually a giant, Paul's physical appearance was not overwhelming. According to a second-century apocryphal writing entitled *The Acts of Paul and Thecla*, a document which perhaps goes back to a first-century writing, Paul's appearance is described. According to this document, Onesiphorus, a resident of Iconium, was to have Paul stay at his house while Paul was visiting that city. This person had known Paul "only in the spirit" and had never "seen him in the flesh." Relying upon a physical description of Paul given to him by Titus, Onesiphorus, his wife, Lectra, and their two children, Simmias and Zeno, "went along the royal road which leads to Lystra" in order to wait for him, looking at all "who came." Eventually they "saw Paul coming, a man small in size, with a bald head and bowlegged, strongly built, with eyebrows meeting and a somewhat hooked and large nose." He was "full of friendliness, for at times he appeared like a man, and at times he had the face of an angel." Here is a rather unflattering account of the first-century Apostle, hence it is thought to be rather accurate! It seems fair to conclude that his physical person was not equal to his spiritual grandeur.

Paul himself seems to give indication of this belief. For example, in his first Epistle to the Corinthians, he writes: "I was with you in weakness and in much fear and trembling; and my speech and my message were not in plausible words of wisdom" (1 Corinthians 2:3-4). In the Second Letter to the Church at Corinth, Paul even quotes the taunt of his opponents when he writes, "For they say, 'His letters are weighty and strong, but his bodily presence is weak, and his speech of no account' " (2 Corinthians 10:10; see also 2:3). Again in the Acts of the Apostles, Paul and Barnabas come to Lystra in Asia Minor where Paul preached the Gospel. After healing a lame man (Acts 14:9-10), the people proclaim that "the gods have come down to us in the likeness of men!" (Acts 14:11). Interestingly enough, Barnabas is referred to as Zeus "and Paul, because he was the chief speaker, they called Hermes." Hermes was known in the Greek pantheon of gods as the eloquent son of Zeus, one not known for his great stature!

Paul's disadvantage in bodily presence was not helped by his vocation. Paul speaks on occasion of his "sufferings." He may have suffered as a journeyman tentmaker, but it is more likely that Paul's references to his sufferings have to do with his proclaiming of the Gospel. At the close of the Epistle to the Galatians, Paul writes, "Henceforth let no man trouble me; for I bear on my body the marks [or stigmata] of Jesus" (6:17; see also Galatians 4:12). This owner's stamp is given elaborate statement in Paul's Second Letter to the Corinth

Church. Little is known about these hardships, but in order to affirm his sufferings as an Apostle, he explains:

[I am a far greater servant of Christ] with far greater labors, far more imprisonments, with countless beatings, and often near death. Five times I have received at the hands of the Jews the forty lashes less one. Three times I have been beaten with rods; once I was stoned. Three times I have been shipwrecked; a night and a day I have been adrift at sea; on frequent journeys, in danger from rivers, danger from robbers, danger from my own people, danger from Gentiles, danger in the city, danger in the wilderness, danger at sea, danger from false brethren; in toil and hardship, through many a sleepness night, in hunger and thirst, often without food, in cold and exposure. And, apart from other things, there is the daily pressure upon me of my anxiety for all the churches (2 Corinthians 11:23-28).

Paul's life experiences give us an interesting and important commentary about life as a Christian. The "experience" may not always be a pleasant one, but the advantages far outweigh the difficulties. Hence Paul could write with enthusiasm, "to live is Christ, and to die is gain" (Philippians 1:21).

Paul experienced a further hindrance, a rather mysterious thing which he referred to as a "thorn in the flesh," or better, "a thorn for the flesh." It is not really known what this ailment could have been, although numerous speculations have been presented over the years.

10

Writing to the Church at Corinth, Paul associates this "painful physical ailment" with his unique experiences of visions and spiritual revelations (2 Corinthians 12:1-9). He indicates that this particular thorn acted as a type of counterbalance, keeping him human and humble. He writes that "elated by the abundance of revelations, a thorn was given me in the flesh, a messenger of Satan, to harass me, to keep me from being too elated" (2 Corinthians 12:7). He goes on to say how he prayed "three times . . . that it should leave me," but Christ's response was, "My grace is sufficient for you, for my power is made perfect in weakness" (2 Corinthians 12:9).

He refers to these revelations as being "caught up to the third heaven — whether in the body or out of the body I do not know, God knows" (verse 2). Paul simply means that his person experienced a nearness of God which cannot be equaled. Little is known about this experience but on this one occasion Paul makes his case. Because his revelations are so sacred that they cannot be told or put into words (verse 4), Paul makes it quite clear that he deserves no credit (verse 5). In fact, he wishes to only boast in his weakness. He concludes saying, "For the sake of Christ, then, I am content with weaknesses, insults, hardships, persecutions, and calamities" (verse 10).

But what is the "thorn for the flesh"? From the Church's saints and theologians, we can find numerous suggestions. St. Chrysostom, Theodoret and Luther understood persecutions; Basil and Tertullian physical illness such as violent headaches; Augustine, Jerome, Aquinas and Calvin believed it to be spiritual temptation. Others have argued that it was carnal temptations, his physical appearance, epilepsy, eye trouble and malarial fever.

Perhaps one of the more probable explanations of

Paul's ailment would be the last one mentioned above: malarial fever. This was a well-known illness in the eastern Mediterranean during Paul's lifetime. A high fever and a severe piercing headache are the main characteristics of this chronic recurring virus that comes upon one when the body is tired and exhausted. But whatever the illness, Paul carried on, relying not upon his own strength but upon the *grace* of Christ. He found he could glory in trouble and adversity ironically because he was strongest when human nature was at its frailest (2 Corinthians 12:8-10).

As a result, Paul's physical limitations and humiliations became in a remarkable way true spiritual strength. He writes to the Corinthians, "If I must boast, I will boast of the things that show my weakness" (2 Corinthians 11:30). Again, referring to his ailment, he writes, "I will all the more gladly boast of my weaknesses, that the power of Christ may rest upon me" (2 Corinthians 12:9-10). Writing to the Galatians, Paul refers to the fact that it was only *because* "of a bodily ailment that I preached the gospel to you at first" (Galatians 4:13). Hence Paul could speak of the eternal treasure of the Gospel which we have "in earthen vessels, to show that the transcendent power belongs to God and not to us. . . . Here indeed we groan . . . we sigh with anxiety" (2 Corinthians 4:7 and 5:2, 4). Paul's character was one that took the weakness of his own physical being and allowed it to be transformed by God's Spirit into true spiritual fiber and strength.

The temperament of his person seems to have been one of nervous vitality and endless energy. How else can we explain his industrious travels and passion for discussion, debate and proclamation? He certainly stirred minds, a personality who could not be confronted with indifference. He must have been a fascinating character electrifying his audiences, who were either deeply moved by his message or were deeply hostile. According to Luke (the probable writer of Acts), after Paul preached in Antioch of Pisidia, the people exited the synogogue and "begged that these things might be told them the next sabbath. And when the meeting of the synagogue broke up, many Jews and devout converts to Judaism followed Paul and Barnabas, who spoke to them and urged them to continue in the grace of God. The next sabbath almost the whole city gathered together to hear the word of God. But when the Jews saw the multitudes, they were filled with jealousy, and contradicted what was spoken by Paul, and reviled him" (Acts 13:42-45). Again, at Iconium, Luke tells us that "the people of the city were divided; some sided with the Jews, and some with the apostles" (Acts 14:4). Paul refers to this polarity of response when he writes to the Corinthians: "We are the aroma of Christ to God among those who are being saved and among those who are perishing, to one a fragrance from death to death, to the other a fragrance from life to life" (2 Corinthians 2:15-16).

Paul's emotional nature, it can be conjectured, had much to do with his eloquence. He appears to have been impulsive, mercurial, demonstrative and passionate — certainly not passive and withdrawing. This is witnessed by his tremendous affection toward his converts. To the Church in Galatia he writes: "My little children, with whom I am again in travail until Christ be formed in you!" (Galatians 4:19). He refers to himself as being "indignant" or distressed, so sensitive was he to the spiritual state of the Corinth Church (2 Corinthians 11:29). To the Thessalonians he states that "we [Paul and Silas; see Acts 16:19-40] were gentle among you, like a nurse taking care of her children. So, being affectionately desirous of you, we were ready to share with you not only the gospel of God but also our own selves, because you had become very dear to us" (1 Thessalonians 2:7-8). In the same letter Paul adds later that "in all our distress and affliction we have been comforted about you through your faith; for now we live, if you stand fast in the Lord" (1 Thessalonians 3:7-8). Throughout Paul's letters he reveals himself as a sensitive, emotional and expressive person, caring deeply and at times anguishing over the needs of his converts.

Paul's letters also indicate an individual who experienced sharp mood changes. In his Epistles to the Galatians, Philippians and 2 Corinthians (as well as in Acts), Paul moves quickly through conflicting feelings of fear and hope, affection and anger mixed with contempt, patience and impatience. On the one hand he can write to the "foolish Galatians" (Galatians 3:1) and on the other hand he tells the Philippians "with tears" that there are enemies of the Christ. Luke tells us that Paul, "filled with the Holy Spirit, looked intently at" the magician Bar-Jesus (Acts 13:9); that he and Barnabas "tore their garments and rushed out among the multitude, crying, 'Men, why are you doing this? We also are men, of like nature with you, and bring you good news' " (Acts 14:14); before Agrippa, Paul "stretched out his hand and made his defense" (Acts 26:1). These instances give us only a minute flash of Paul's person, yet they indicate to us his zeal for the Gospel, his lively emotional state and his animated character. He spoke from the heart and he appealed to the heart.

We must be reminded that although we seek to catch a glimpse of his personality, he attributed all his successes and effectiveness as an Apostle to the Spirit of Christ. Here was the energy that enabled Christ to speak through him (2 Corinthians 13:3). To the Colossians he wrote: "For this I toil, striving with all the energy which he mightily inspires within me" (Colossians 1:29). To the Thessalonians he wrote: "Our gospel came to you not only in word [Paul, Silas and Timothy], but also in power and in the Holy Spirit and with full conviction" (1 Thessalonians 1:5). Paul was a person of the largest spiritual capacity filled with the Holy Spirit of Christ.

It cannot be ignored that Paul experienced spiritual gifts. The Greek word *"charismata"* is used to describe these gifts based upon the grace (or the *charis*, Greek for grace) of God. These "gifts" were experienced by prominent Old Testament figures, by John the Baptist, and of course by Jesus — where the charisma is greatest (Luke 2:40); by the Apostles after Pentecost (Acts 2) and by Christians since the first century. Paul clearly exercised miraculous powers. He cast a devil out of Elymas (Acts 13:9-11), he healed a lame man (Acts 14:9-10) and he instructed one parish not to protect a person from Satan's destructive powers (1 Corinthians 5:4-5; see also 1 Corinthians 4:19-21).

Paul, however, is careful to note that these miraculous signs are not the true mark of the Apostle. The real indication of apostleship is the enduring and lasting work of God through God's instrument — rather than the brief, the flashy and the instantaneous. To the congregation at Corinth he writes, "Are we beginning to commend ourselves again? Or do we need, as some do, letters of recommendation to you, or from you? You yourselves are our letter of recommendation, written on your hearts, to be known and read by all men; and you show that you are a letter from Christ delivered by us, written not with ink but with the Spirit of the living God, not on tablets of stone but on tablets of human hearts" (2 Corinthians 3:1-3). For Paul the Christian faith was a way of life that could include the miraculous, the unusual, the glorious moment (such as an experience of the third heaven, 2 Corinthians 12:2-4). But more matter-of-factly, it was a way of life in Christ that has as its essence the telling of the Good News (either in word or in life-style) and the growing into Christ. This was a long-term, life-committing process.

Paul also spoke in tongues. He indicates that he did so "more than most," but clearly he downplayed this gift as being less than vital for the spiritual growth of all. Again to the Corinthians he wrote, ". . . in church I would rather speak five words with my mind, in order to instruct others, than ten thousand words in a tongue." He goes on to add that "tongues are a sign not for believers but for unbelievers" (1 Corinthians 14:18-22). As indicated above, Paul also had "visions and revelations of the Lord," and had been "caught up into Paradise" hearing "things that cannot be told" (2 Corinthians 12:1-4). But for Paul, all this spiritual dynamism was secondary to the living God, the Lord Jesus Christ, who sent the Holy Spirit into our midst that we might be guided toward a fullness of Christ that becomes a gateway to eternity.

If we could uncover one fault in the personality of Paul the Apostle that is evident in his letters and in the Acts of the Apostles, it would have to be his impetuousness. In his dealings with congregations and individuals, his sense of urgency and forcefulness could trigger a heated temper and hasty words that were later regretted. This is exemplified in Paul's impatience with Mark, caused by Mark's desire to go no further on their missionary journey (a stubbornness perhaps instigated by the controversy of Jews and Gentiles eating together).

Luke records that "there arose a sharp contention, so that they separated from each other" (Acts 15:39 and 13:13). This "contention" was later rectified (see Colossians 4:10 where "Mark the cousin of Barnabas" and others are "a comfort" to Paul while under house arrest in Rome). Luke records that Paul calls the high priest Ananias a "whitewashed wall," only to retract his statement moments later saying, "I did not know, brethren, that he was the high priest; for it is written, 'You shall not speak evil of a ruler of your people'" (Acts 23:5). Writing to the Galatians, Paul blurts out, "I wish those who unsettle you would mutilate themselves," a bitter remark (Galatians 5:12). Again to the Corinth Church he hastily comments, "For even if I made you sorry with my letter, I do not regret it (though I did regret it), for I see that the letter grieved you, though only for a while" (2 Corinthians 7:8).

This impulsiveness, or explosiveness, of Paul's character is in accord with other words that have been used to describe his person. We have noted he was sensitive, passionate, experiential, capable of religious ecstasy, courageous, volatile and fiery. Here was the exciting individual — a true personality, who was called to take the message of Christ to the Gentile world.

To be sure, these few instances — mainly from Paul's letters — offer only a hazy mosaic of his person. We can imagine him to have been full of life, effervescent for the Gospel of Christ. He was an intellectual giant who colorfully articulated and interpreted morally the Christian way and the Christian faith. A man of the heart, he could cry and rejoice, responding to the situations he faced taking the Gospel to the Gentiles. His intense preoccupation with the Gospel is an invaluable and eternal witness to the meaning of Christian commitment and devotion, a vocation to which every Christian is called.

Hence we begin to catch a glimpse of the person behind the letters. Now we can turn our attention to his life's activities.

• The Historical Life of Paul

Stephen the Martyr

We shall begin with Stephen. This early Christian martyr offers the first window through which we catch a glimpse of Paul. We would not be on hollow ground in assuming that Stephen's martyrdom became, in the hands of God, an important event in the life of Paul. So let us peer through this window first.

Stephen was undoubtedly a true spiritual trailblazer for first-century Christians. Stephen, whose name in Greek means *"crown,"* gave his life as a witness to the Good News of Jesus the Christ. His action was a true omen of things to come for the young and unexpecting followers of Jesus. Stephen gave his apologia before the Sanhedrin (Acts 7), declaring the end of the twin Judaic religious foundations, the temple and the Torah.

Perhaps Stephen, having more of a Hellenistic background, was better able to grasp the true meaning of Jesus' teachings about the kingdom of God (see Luke 16:16, 13:35, Mark 13:32 and Matthew 5:21-48). Stephen would have been less inhibited by the "kingdom of Israel" attitude (Acts 1:6), and unlike the first Apostles was better able to see the revolutionary meaning of Jesus' teachings and person. So after retelling the story of God's relationship with Israel from Abraham up to the then current setting in Israel, he indicates the people's deafness and disobedience to God's purpose.

In many ways, Stephen's testimony is an anticipation of Paul's preaching and message that would soon follow. Drawing upon Old Testament Scripture, he directed his listeners beyond the temple and the Torah, or law. He indicates how the great and lasting portions of Israel's past is based upon men of vision who responded to the call of God, telling of a future prophet or deliverer. Always in

18

the past Israel has rejected God's Spirit and now they have topped all their sins by putting to death God's holy one, the Messiah, Jesus. It is no wonder his listeners were extremely angered at what they heard and made preparations to stone this "slanderer." Perhaps Paul was among the debaters in the synagogue who attempted to argue with Stephen.

Stephen understood Jesus' message. But Stephen clearly perceived that the kingdom which Jesus spoke of meant, in the end, elimination of Jewish privilege and triggered a new universal kingdom of God.

Three aspects of Stephen's martyrdom are worthy of note.

First, as Stephen is stoned to death in the gruesome traditional fashion (Deuteronomy 13:6-11), for serving other gods, he prays for those to whom he has just spoken, those who are in the process of executing him. Luke vividly tells us that "he prayed, 'Lord Jesus, receive my spirit.' And he knelt down and cried with a loud voice, 'Lord, do not hold this sin against them.' And when he had said this, he fell asleep" (Acts 7:59-60). According to Luke, Stephen spoke and acted as his Master. In Luke's first volume of Christianity, that is, his Gospel witnessing the life and events surrounding Jesus, he records that Jesus said from the cross, "Father, forgive them; for they know not what they do" (Luke 23:34). Stephen had understood well Jesus' life and His significance for the new kingdom of God.

Second, Luke writes that "full of the Holy Spirit, [Stephen] gazed into heaven and saw the glory of God, and Jesus standing at the right hand of God; and he said, 'Behold, I see the heavens opened, and the Son of man standing at the right hand of God' " (Acts 7:55-56). Stephen saw a vision as he gave his witness about Jesus. It is important to notice that as danger drew increasingly near, as those to whom he spoke became "enraged, and they ground their teeth against him" (Acts 7:54), like Jesus in the Garden of Gethsemane, Stephen is not distracted. Nor is Stephen abandoned in his time of trial. Then they charged him, dragged him out of the city and executed him.

It is worth noting how Stephen refers to Jesus. His vision glimpses the "Son of man" (Acts 7:56). This is the only time this title is used, with the exception of Jesus' own reference to himself. Jesus probably uses the phrase based on Daniel 7:13ff, where the Son of man is exalted to God in the heavens and is given "dominion and glory and kingdom, that all peoples, nations, and languages should serve him; his dominion is an everlasting dominion, which shall not pass away, and his kingdom one that shall not be destroyed" (Daniel 7:14). Stephen seems to have not only a personal vision in the midst of his own imminent death, but he also seems to perceive Jesus' sovereignty over all nations. The Jewish people wanted to retain their old customs, but Stephen saw a vision of a Christ who was Lord of the world. In fact, Stephen's witness has some clear affinity to the New Testament book of Hebrews, where we read: "Therefore let us go forth to him [Jesus] outside the camp [of Israel], bearing abuse for him. For here we have no lasting city, but we seek the city which is to come [the kingdom of God]" (Hebrews 13:13-14). Stephen's vision and the theme of the homily to the Hebrews were realized in Paul's missionary efforts to the Gentiles. Paul writes to the Galatians, "[God] was pleased to reveal his Son to me, in order that I might preach him among the Gentiles" (Galatians 1:16). Stephen's vision became the substance and goal of Paul's work.

Nevertheless, Stephen's example is clear. The person who is not distracted to look elsewhere, the one who keeps his concentrated gaze upon the Christ, will not be abandoned in his time of trial, but will in fact be given strength to do things which would otherwise be *humanly impossible*. This certainly is true for Stephen in facing death, something all must experience. Yet here the coming of death is easily surmountable simply because the peace of God came upon Stephen in those last moments, the peace that comes upon the one who has done the right thing with his life even if that thing has led to death. In the midst of a violent death Stephen is at peace, and so Luke states rather elegantly, "he fell asleep" (Acts 7:60).

The third aspect of Stephen's death is the clear and consenting presence of Saul. Luke tells us that as "they cast him out of the city and stoned him . . . the witnesses laid down their garments at the feet of a young man named Saul" (Acts 7:58). St. Augustine later wrote: "If Stephen had not prayed, the church would not have had Paul." We can assume with some certainty that Paul never forgot the fearless faith of Stephen. Here was a great martyr of the Christian faith who bore witness to the tradition that the blood of these people became the seed of the Church. Many have argued that it was Paul's experience of witnessing Stephen's martyrdom that set the stage for his conversion to Christianity on the Damascus road. Perhaps it was during his travels on this road that he suddenly realized that Stephen was right, the crucified Jesus of Nazareth was the Lord from heaven. This conversion was to change the entire world and it is to this event we must now turn.

Paul's Conversion

Paul understood his experience on the Damascus road as the turning point of his life. All his future interests and his interpretations of the Christian faith relate to this event. It is interesting that Paul refers to this experience as a revelation. To the Galatians he writes, God "was pleased to reveal his Son to me" (Galatians 1:16) and to the Church at Corinth he states how Jesus "appeared to James, then to all the apostles. Last of all . . . he appeared also to me" (1 Corinthians 15:7-8). For Paul, the revelation that Jesus was resurrected and exalted translated into an about-face of his life — a radical change that transformed a very Jewish and upright young man into a dedicated and tremendously intense follower and Apostle of Jesus.

Paul's experience is described three times by Luke in the Book of Acts, indicating its importance for the eary Church. Luke summarizes what happened in Acts 9:3-19; Paul tells what happened to a Jewish mob in Jerusalem in 22:6-16; and Paul gives a further account in 26:9-13 in his defense before Herod Agrippa II. These accounts are in very close agreement — but of course, because the contextual circumstances of each account differ, we would not expect them to be identical. We can piece together the experience something like the following.

Paul was a young man (according to Acts 7:58) at the martyrdom of Stephen, probably indicating an age between twenty-four and forty. It is more likely that Paul was at the younger end of this range. He was more than likely a rather influential Pharisee who, by his own confession, was highly motivated in the Jewish faith. He writes to the Galatians, "For you have heard of my former life in Judaism, how I persecuted the church of God violently and tried to destroy it; and I advanced in Judaism beyond many of my own age among my people, so extremely zealous was I for the traditions of my fathers" (Galatians 1:13-14). Before Herod Agrippa II, while defending himself, he indicates in some detail the extent of his zeal:

> *I myself was convinced that I ought to do many things in opposing the name of Jesus of Nazareth. And I did so in Jerusalem; I not only shut up many of the saints in prison, by authority from the chief priests, but when they were put to death I cast my vote against them. And I punished them often in all the synagogues and tried to make them blaspheme; and in raging fury against them, I persecuted them even to foreign cities (Acts 26:9-11).*

Hence it was only proper that he hold the garments at Stephen's execution.

One of the cities where the fanatic followers of Jesus were beginning to congregate was Damascus. In times past, religious refugees had fled to this city (about 130 B.C.) indicating not only that it was a city of religious tolerance but now a prime location for telling the message of the resurrected Jesus. So Paul went to the high priest requesting a letter that would allow him to seek out the Christians in Damascus and bring them back to Jerusalem for trial. Luke tells us that after Stephen's death, the Christians continued to proclaim the message that Jesus was alive (see Acts 8).

As a result, Paul, "still breathing threats and murder against the disciples of the Lord, went to the high priest and asked him for letters to the synagogues at Damascus, so that if he found any belonging to the Way [that is, Christians], men or women, he might bring them bound to Jerusalem" (Acts 9:1-2). Paul would have begun a rather lengthy journey — travel time of about one week — at a distance of not much less than two hundred miles. Paul would have walked alone because he was a Pharisee, although he had traveling companions, probably officials from the Sanhedrin. It was toward the end of his journey, about noonday, as he approached Damascus (Acts 9:3), indicating a rather desolate and lonely section of road passing through arid and dry countryside, when the experience occurs.

The account is portrayed in very dramatic language. Luke states that "suddenly a light from heaven flashed about him. And he fell to the ground and heard a voice" (Acts 9:3-4). Paul describes it as a "great light from heaven" (Acts 22:6), "brighter than the sun" (Acts 26:13). The voice says to him, "Saul, Saul, why do you persecute me?" (Acts 9:4; 22:7; 26:14). Paul responds with a question: "Who are you, Lord?" The response is given: "I am Jesus, whom you are persecuting" (Acts 9:5; 22:8; 26:15).

According to the one account (Acts 22:10), Paul asks a second question, "What shall I do, Lord?" Paul is then given instructions to go into Damascus. He discovers he has lost his eyesight, "so they led him by the hand and brought him into Damascus" (Acts 9:8). In Damascus lived a Christian by the name of Ananias who was also given a vision by the Lord. Ananias is told to "rise and go to the street called Straight, and inquire in the house of Judas for a man of Tarsus named Saul [or Paul]" (Acts 9:11). Ananias goes, lays his hands on Paul and says, " 'Brother Saul, receive your sight.' And in that very hour I received my sight and saw him" (Acts 22:13). Shortly thereafter, he received a further vision when the Lord said to him, "I will send you far away to the Gentiles" (Acts 22:21; see also verses 17-20) because his life was in danger round and about Jerusalem.

Some scholars see this Damascus road experience as more a surrender than a conversion. That is to say, some argue that Paul, having been influenced by his rabbi-tutor Gamaliel, a possible sympathizer with the follow-ers of Jesus, and having been influenced by the martyr-dom of Stephen, was in fact quite thoughtful about things. It was not until the Damascus road episode that Paul fi-nally surrendered. However it is perceived, one thing is certainly clear; from this time onward Paul is an intense and devoted worker who counts himself as one of the Apostles. He even changes his name, from the Jewish hero and famous king of his tribe, Saul, to the Roman sur-name Paul. This may well have been caused by his under-standing that he should become a proclaimer of Christ to the Gentiles, hence he would use his Roman or Latin name for the Gentile community and his Hebrew name for the Jewish community. Nevertheless, a great change occurs on the Damascus road, the result being a new direction *and* a different name.

One aspect of Paul's conversion experience is of par-ticular importance — that is the overwhelming bright light. In the New Testament, this is a common designa-tion for Jesus Christ. (In the Old Testament, God is de-scribed as light; see Isaiah 10:17; 51:4; 60:3; Wisdom 7:26; and others.) For example, in John's Gospel we read: "In him was life, and the life was the light of men" (1:4; see also verses 5 and 9). Again in the Gospel of John, where the designation of Jesus as light is common and frequent, we read: ". . . the light has come into the world, and men loved darkness rather than light" (3:19; see also 8:12, 9:5 and 12:46). In the first Epistle of John, which may be associated with the author of the Gospel of John, we read "God is light, and in him is no darkness at all" (1 John 1:5). This is followed by the author's refer-ence to Jesus Christ in that "the darkness is passing away and the true light is already shining" (1 John 2:8).

Light then is employed in the Scriptures to signify

the revelation of God. Luke, quoting the Prophet Malachi (4:2), states that Jesus is literally the rising sun; "the day shall dawn upon us from on high to give light to those who sit in darkness and in the shadow of death, to guide our feet into the way of peace" (Luke 1:78-79). Throughout John's Gospel, *light* is inseparable from *life, truth* and *love*. But what did this all mean for Paul?

The surrendering experience of Paul to the "light of the world" introduced him into the wonderful *tension* of living as a follower of the exalted Christ. Paul slowly came to realize that the beginning of the *tension* in the Christian life was salvation which meant the turning from sin to grace and from darkness to light. So Paul went to the Gentiles "to open their eyes, that they may turn from darkness to light" (Acts 26:18; see also 13:47). He writes to the Ephesians, ". . . once you were darkness, but now you are light in the Lord" (Ephesians 5:8). To the Christians at Thessalonica he exhorted, "For you are all sons of light and sons of the day . . . keep awake and be sober" (1 Thessalonians 5:5-6). To the Corinth community he says, "For it is the God who said, 'Let light shine out of darkness,' who has shone in our hearts to give the light of the knowledge of the glory of God in the face of Christ" (2 Corinthians 4:6). For Paul, salvation, or *salvatio* (soteriology), has to do with light and grace *here and now*. (See the writer of Hebrews' use of the word enlightened for those who have experienced *salvatio*: 6:4 and 10:32.)

The second part of the *tension* of the Christian life is that of the future. For Paul, his vision of the exalted Lord came to mean that we have already been delivered from the power of darkness and translated into the power of light, but the full future divine light and grace is yet to come. The *tension* is intensified by the *salvatio* that is well in progress *now* and the future return of the exalted

Christ. Hence, with regard to the kingdom of God well in progress, he encourages the Church at Colossae to give "thanks to the Father, who has qualified us [or you] to share in the inheritance of the saints in light. He has delivered us from the dominion of darkness and transferred us to the kingdom of his beloved Son, in whom we have redemption" (Colossians 1:12-14). For Paul, "the night is far gone, the day is at hand" (Romans 13:12).

With regard to the future fullness of the kingdom, Paul writes to those at Philippi, "But our commonwealth is in heaven, and from it we await a Savior, the Lord Jesus Christ, who will change our lowly body to be like his glorious body, by the power which enables him even to subject all things to himself" (Philippians 3:20-21). This dynamic tension in Paul's life, stemming from the Damascus road experience, is again addressed in his later letter to the Corinthian Church: "We all, with unveiled face, beholding the glory of the Lord, are being changed into his likeness from one degree of glory to another; for this comes from the Lord who is the Spirit" (2 Corinthians 3:18; see also 4:7-5:5). In effect, for Paul, the end of the age is uncertain, but the *future* is certain!

This vision of the exalted Christ makes Paul's thought dynamic and alive. Behind all his letters is a *living person*. His writings have only the one focusing purpose: to direct individuals toward the living Christ. This living person is the exciting *tension* at the center of the Christian life: He has come and He will come again.

Paul's Background

What can we know about the chronology of Paul's life? On the basis of two sources, we can piece together approximate dates, movements and general developments in Paul's pre-conversion and post-conversion life. Of course, we can assume no accuracy simply because

Paul left no journal or diary of his life. Yet the two sources, Luke's second volume, the Acts of the Apostles and Paul's occasional personal testimonies found in his letters give us a somewhat adequate picture of the first Christian theologian and Gospel interpreter.

Of the two sources just mentioned, we could entitle Luke's first volume of his two-volume work (the *Gospel of Luke* and the *Acts of the Apostles*), "Jesus and His Followers." In the first volume, Luke is telling us of Jesus' life. He states at the beginning of his Gospel the careful research and purpose of his writing:

> *Inasmuch as many have undertaken to compile a narrative of the things which have been accomplished among us, just as they were delivered to us by those who from the beginning were eyewitnesses and ministers of the word, it seemed good to me also, having followed all things closely for some time past, to write an orderly account for you, most excellent Theophilus, that you may know the truth concerning the things of which you have been informed (Luke 1:1-4).*

Although the identity of Theophilus is not clear, Luke's purpose for writing the first volume cannot be questioned.

Luke's second volume is of great importance because it is the only attempted historical account of first-century Christianity. Establishing the date of Acts has been of great interest because of the book's historical importance. It would seem that the second volume of Luke's study was written during the early 60s, completed not long before Paul's trial and eventual martyrdom. Having a more Jewish orientation than was first thought,

Luke seems to be intent upon *persuasion*, that is, persuading the various Jewish communities that the Christians have the truth (rather than the Jews) and explaining how the Jewish faith has gotten into such a conflict.

Luke does not want to tear the young Churches apart through *confrontation* between Jews and Christians. He desires to persuade all to stop their squabbling and fall in place behind Paul, who is about to go on trial in Rome. Luke indicates at the beginning of his writings the dominant themes he will pursue: the coming of the Holy Spirit (Acts 1:2 and 5) and the coming of the kingdom of God (Acts 1:3). Luke also includes Jesus' last conversation with the disciples just prior to the ascension (Acts 1:6-10). There he states that the disciples are not to worry about the "time or season" of the kingdom, that they (and not Israel) will be given the power of the Spirit, and that they were to witness throughout the inhabited world. For Luke, the dominant personality in these divine historical events is Paul of Tarsus.

The other source that we have of Paul's life is his letters. Although Paul is not interested in telling of himself, on occasion the establishing of his own authority before those who would challenge his leadership required some autobiography. These sections are brief and rare, but firsthand. The best example is the Letter to the Galatians, where Paul is pressed to justify his authority which is apparently being challenged (1:11-2:10). In order to vindicate his apostleship, he explains how he received the Gospel (1:11-12) and offers some background information in order to show the contrast between what he was and what he now is (1:13-2:10) — all centered around his conversion experience. (For other autobiographical material, see, for example, Philippians 3:5-6; 1 Corinthians 16:5-8; 2 Corinthians 2:9-13; 11:32-33; Romans 15:22-28.)

By way of these two sources then, we can approximately summarize Paul's life and movements, noting that there has been very little agreement among scholars with regard to exact dates and general movements. However, some archeological discoveries have presented useful information: Roman administrative appointments (the proconsulship of Gallio in Achaia, Acts 18:12); the eastern Mediterranean famine during the reign of Emperor Claudius (Acts 11:28-30), and the edict of Claudius expelling the Jews from Rome because of their constant fighting over Christ (see Acts 18:2). These pinpoint some details of Paul's life so that a fair chronology can be loosely constructed.

Paul was probably born sometime during the first decade of the first century. (As noted, he was a "young man" at Stephen's death, Acts 7:58.) He was born in Tarsus, the capital of Cilicia (Acts 22:3), an area on the eastern edge of modern-day Turkey. Situated twenty-five kilometers from the Mediterranean Sea and at the base of the Taurus mountains, Tarsus was a center of Hellenistic culture (that is, conformity to Greek ways, especially Greek language) and a major city in Asia Minor. It must have been an exciting place to live, being the center of government for the province of Cilicia, a center of trade and learning. Two references from the New Testament (Acts 17:28 and Titus 1:12) indicate that Paul was schooled in Greek literature and culture. In both these places he quotes freely from the Greek poets Epimenides and Aratus, not a common practice for one outside of Hellenism.

Paul was born of a Jewish family that traced its heritage back to the tribe of Benjamin (Romans 11:1 and Philippians 3:5), and from his birth was a Roman citizen (Acts 22:25-29; 16:37; 23:27). He had at least one sister, indicated by the assistance given Paul in the face of a

Jewish plot. Luke records that "the son of Paul's sister heard of their ambush; so he went and entered the barracks and told Paul" (Acts 23:16).

Paul's Roman citizenship was a coveted and prestigious status for a foreign person. Hence, when Paul is about to be scourged or beaten, he asks the centurion, "Is it lawful for you to scourge a man who is a Roman citizen, and uncondemned?" The centurion immediately went to his superior, the tribune, and said, "What are you about to do? For this man is a Roman citizen." The tribune then goes to Paul and tells him that in fact he had bought his citizenship "for a large sum." Paul responds, "But I was *born* a citizen." Luke then records: "So those who were about to examine him withdrew from him instantly; and the tribune also was afraid, for he realized that Paul was a Roman citizen and that he had bound him" (Acts 22:29). Roman citizens, unlike other individuals, were protected from scourging as long as they were uncondemned. Such was the enviable status of citizenship (see also Acts 16:37 and 23:27).

Although the degree of importance has yet to be established, the influence of the Greek culture upon Paul is significant. Where Jesus used examples from nature and rural country life for His teachings, Paul uses all types of Greek terms and ideas. For example, to the Church at Philippi he draws an analogy between the Greek games (modern-day Olympic games) and the Christian life. He encourages the Philippian believers to hold "fast the word of life, so that in the day of Christ I may be proud that I did not run in vain" (Philippians 2:16), and to "press on toward the goal for the prize of the upward call of God in Christ Jesus" (3:14). He uses a Greek political term when he refers to the Christian's "commonwealth" in heaven (Philippians 3:20; see also 1:27 and Ephesians 2:19). Paul can also be found making use of Greek commercial terminology (Philemon 18; Colossians 2:14) and legal terms (Galatians 3:15, 4:1-2; Romans 7:1ff). Clearly Paul was in touch with the world in which he lived and he used the current fabric of terminology to communicate the Gospel of Jesus Christ.

Exactly when Paul left Tarsus and went to Jerusalem is uncertain. Some have argued that he left Tarsus at a very young age in order to be educated by Gamaliel, the well-known rabbi in Jerusalem (Acts 22:3). Others argue that Paul's letters reveal traces of Greek education, indicating that he came to Jerusalem at a later age. Paul, defending himself before King Agrippa against the accusations of the Jews, states that, "My manner of life from my youth, spent from the beginning among my own nation and at Jerusalem, is known by all the Jews . . . according to the strictest party of our religion I have lived as a Pharisee" (Acts 26:4-5; see also Acts 22:3 where Paul again states he was brought up in Jerusalem). To the believers at Galatia he wrote, "I advanced in Judaism beyond many of my own age among my people, so extremely zealous was I for the traditions of my fathers" (Galatians 1:14).

Paul was also trained in tentmaking. This was not unusual for a rabbi-teacher. They often had to acquire a practical trade in order to support their "higher" calling. This would seem an appropriate trade for Paul because it is a basic profession for the life of many in the Near East, even to this day. Nomads (those with no fixed land who move through the more arid sections of the territory), shepherds and soldiers all used the tent as their basic mode of housing. Not only was there a need for tents, but in the city of Paul's birth, Tarsus, a well-known goat-hair cloth was produced which was used for tentmaking. Paul did find some fellowship in this trade. According to Luke, when Paul was at Corinth, he met

Aquila and Priscilla "and because he was of the same trade he stayed with them, and they worked, for by trade they were tentmakers" (Acts 18:3).

Not knowing exactly when Paul came to Jerusalem, we must not fail to notice his motivation. He came to train as a Pharisee and so become a rabbi, a teacher of the Jewish law. He apparently was on the rise, having already achieved some status in this profession because of his "official" journey to Damascus. He may even have been a member of the Sanhedrin, the council or court of justice that ruled Israel. Luke records that Paul "not only shut up many of the saints in prison, by authority from the chief priests, but when they were put to death I cast my vote against them" (Acts 26:10). According to rabbinical tradition, the Sanhedrin was originally created by Moses (Numbers 11:16) and therefore carried powerful status.

If Paul was ordained a rabbi, he would have had to have been at least forty years of age. This was the required age for ordination. It would follow then that his conversion would have occurred in middle age. Furthermore, if Paul was a rabbi, he would have been married. Marriage was a requirement for all rabbis. So perhaps when Paul wrote to the Church at Corinth, "To the unmarried and the widows I say that it is well for them to remain single as I do" (1 Corinthians 7:8), he was putting himself in the category of the widowed. But because Paul's ordination is uncertain, neither his age nor his marital status can be accurately determined — so we are left to mere speculation.

Paul's Apostleship

After the monumental event of Paul's conversion experience, which we have already considered, we find Paul in Damascus (Acts 9:10-19 and 22:12-16). After Ananias's visit to Paul, the new convert gained his sight, "then he rose and was baptized, and took food and was strengthened. For several days he was with the disciples at Damascus" (Acts 9:18-20). Paul carried out his plans to visit the synagogues of the city, but with a most unexpected message. Suddenly, the very faith he came to eliminate was proclaimed! What a turn of events! (Acts 9:20-25).

In the Epistle to the Galatians Paul mentions a journey to "Arabia," most likely meaning a territory just east of Damascus (Galatians 1:17-18). This sojourn has been the target of much speculation, including everything from visiting Mt. Sinai to visiting with the Essenes (an ascetic Jewish sect that lived in the wilderness). This visit to the wilderness most likely took place during his stay in Damascus. According to the most sensible estimates, Paul's stay in Damascus totaled about three years. If Paul's conversion experience occurred within one to two years after the crucifixion, Paul would have left Damascus about A.D. 37, depending of course on the year Christ was crucified.

Paul was so "shocking" in his proclamations at Damascus synagogues that "the Jews plotted to kill him" (Acts 9:23). Eventually, as the Jews watched the gates, Paul was taken "by night and let . . . down over the wall, lowering him in a basket" (Acts 9:25). Where would the new Apostle go after his escape?

Luke tells us he went to Jerusalem, but the disciples "were all afraid of him, for they did not believe that he was a disciple" (Acts 9:26; see also Galatians 1:18-24 which is probably the same visit). Such was Paul's early reputation in and around Jerusalem! If the disciples were terrified by him — how angered the Pharisees must have been, rabbis and members of the Sanhedrin! At this point we are told that Barnabas intervenes, and Paul begins "preaching boldly in the name of the Lord" in Jerusalem (Acts 9:29). Paul's daring and courageous proclamation again placed his life in jeopardy and we are told that the "brethren . . . brought him down to Caesarea, and sent him off to Tarsus" (Acts 9:30). Caesarea is a coastal town northwest of Jerusalem and Paul was possibly put on a ship bound for his "home city," Tarsus.

While in Jerusalem, Paul is eventually able to visit with the disciples where he "saw none of the other apostles except James the Lord's brother." Paul indicates to the Galatians that his primary purpose for traveling to Jerusalem was to meet Peter. Paul stayed with Peter (and perhaps James) for fifteen days — what an important and crucial meeting (Galatians 1:18-24)! It also seems likely that Paul experienced a state of ecstasy or a trance while at prayer in the Temple (Acts 22:17) during this visit to Jerusalem. In this trance Paul is told to "Make haste and get quickly out of Jerusalem, because they will not accept your testimony about me" (verse 18). He apparently did not meet many of the other believers in Jerusalem, but certainly they knew him by reputation. Now Paul was beginning to build a different and everlasting reputation.

From the time Paul went to Tarsus, and for approximately the next ten years, very little is known about his activities. He himself states that he was involved in proclaiming the Good News of the Gospel, evangelizing where possible. Later Paul could write to the Galatians that it was heard said, "He who once persecuted us is now preaching the faith he once tried to destroy" (Galatians 1:23). Perhaps it was during these years that he endured the imprisonments, numerous beatings, shipwrecks, lack of food and shelter that he speaks of in 2 Corinthians 11:22-27. It also seems likely that Paul probably experienced his "visions and revelations of the Lord" (see 2 Corinthians 12:1-4). He writes to the Church at

Corinth that his experience of the third heaven happened fourteen years ago, about the time Paul was active as a "missionary" in and around the region of Tarsus.

After these silent years, we find Paul being called by Barnabas to Antioch. This city was very cosmopolitan, very Hellenistic, a center for commerce and a political capital. It is on the Orontes River, some twenty-five kilometers from the Mediterranean Sea. (It is the modern-day city of Antakya in the Hatay province of Turkey.) The third largest Roman city in Paul's time, it had a population of approximately two hundred thousand. It was densely populated, the place of much "religious" activity, including Hellenistic proselytizing Jews (attempting to convert the Gentiles) and the proclaimers of Christ who had left Jerusalem in order to evangelize and convert others (see Acts 11:19-26).

Because of the success of the missionary effort there, the Church in Jerusalem "sent Barnabas to Antioch" (verse 22). Luke then tells us that "when he came and saw the grace of God, he was glad; and he exhorted them all to remain faithful to the Lord with steadfast purpose. . . . So Barnabas went to Tarsus to look for Saul; and when he found him, he brought him to Antioch" (Acts 11:23-26).

It is interesting that here in Antioch the word "Christian" first appears as a designation of Jesus' followers. The title is given by the Gentiles to those who are adherents of Christ (the personal name with a Latin suffix, *ianus*). Luke writes that "in Antioch the disciples were for the first time called Christians" (Acts 11:26). Christianity had now made an important transition, from a rural religious movement to a significant religion within an important cosmopolitan city — and Paul was right in the middle leading the way.

After one year in Antioch (Acts 11:26), two things

happen. First, a prophet named Agabus comes to Antioch from Jerusalem "and foretold by the Spirit that there would be a great famine over all the world . . . the disciples determined, every one according to his ability, to send relief to the brethren who lived in Judea" (Acts 11:28-29). So an offering was taken by Barnabas and Paul to Jerusalem. Second, persecutions of the Christians broke out under Herod Agrippa I. James the brother of John was executed and Peter was imprisoned (Acts 12). So when Paul and Barnabas come to Jerusalem, they visit with the Church leaders in private. Their stay must have been very brief, and the approximate date for this visit would be about the year 45 or 46.

After this journey, things begin to move more quickly. Luke simply states that "Barnabas and Saul [Paul] returned from Jerusalem when they had fulfilled their mission, bringing with them John whose other name was Mark" (Acts 12:25). A message from the Holy Spirit during worship called Barnabas and Saul (Paul) to a special work. The community of Christians "after fasting and praying . . . laid their hands on them and sent them off" (Acts 13:3). This was the *first missionary* journey of Paul who, being led by the Spirit (Acts 13:4), proclaimed the message of Christ on Cyprus (Barnabas's home country) and then on to Asia Minor, modern-day Turkey. The outward journey established congregations and the return journey allowed them to visit each new community (with the exception of bypassing Cyprus on their return to Antioch). In each town, Barnabas and Paul began their work with the Jewish synagogue but directed their message to both Jews and Gentiles. They returned to Antioch about A.D. 47 or 48.

Although there were many converts, trouble was on the horizon. Messengers from the Jerusalem Church arrived in Antioch and made it a point to visit some of the new churches in Asia Minor. They argued that Paul had only half the truth, and that the Old Testament and Jewish practices had to be adopted if one was to become a true convert or follower of Jesus Christ (Acts 15:1-2). These individuals came to be known as Judaizers, those who would "Judaize" the Christian faith. The new Christians were confused and some sought to keep the Jewish laws and practices. When Paul learned of this he was extremely angry. Because Paul could not visit these churches, he wrote to them — the Letter to the Galatians. (Throughout this study, we will not make a distinction between letter and epistle and will use the terms interchangeably.)

Hence Luke tells us that the debate between the Judaizers and the Gentile mission became so intense that "Paul and Barnabas and some of the others were appointed to go up to Jerusalem to the apostles and the elders about this question" (Acts 15:2). The problem was simply whether one had to become a Jew before becoming a Christian. The church leaders in Jerusalem were practicing Jews and asked if Gentile converts should be circumcised.

A "meeting" took place in Jerusalem, probably about 48 or 49. This is known as the first "apostolic council" of the Church. The general debate that took place is recorded for us in Acts 15 (see also Galatians 2). The concluding agreements of the council followed the advice of Peter: no circumcision required nor adherence to the Mosaic law. The Church was now free from its roots and could rely fully upon the person Jesus Christ.

After Paul and the Antioch party returned to their city, Peter paid them a visit. At first, Peter ate with Gentile converts. This was the practice of Paul but was not the normal custom for a Jew. When Peter was rebuked by conservative Jews from Judea (Galatians 2:12), he changed his ways and convinced Barnabas to do the same. Paul was furious! He wrote later: "But when Cephas [Peter] came to Antioch I opposed him to his face, because he stood condemned. For before certain men came from James, he ate with the Gentiles; but when they came he drew back and separated himself, fearing the circumcision party" (Galatians 2:11-12; see also verses 13-14). Such was Paul's enthusiasm and commitment to Christ and the Gospel.

After the confrontation between Peter and Paul, Luke tells us that "Paul and Barnabas remained in Antioch, teaching and preaching the word of the Lord, with many others also" (Acts 15:35). Paul then requests Barnabas to return with him to "visit every city where we proclaimed the word of the Lord, and see how they are" (Acts 15:36). Barnabas agrees, but wishes to take his cousin John (Mark) with them. Paul thought the contrary because he had not proven a help on the first missionary journey and had gone back early deserting Paul and Barnabas. After an argument, Barnabas took Mark and sailed to Cyprus and Paul chose Silas to accompany him on his visits to the churches in Asia Minor (Acts 15:36-41).

Paul's *second missionary* journey (between the years 49 to 51 or 52), takes him through Asia Minor to the Aegean Sea. He visited such places as Philippi, Thessalonica, Corinth and Athens in Greece. On the outward journey, he visited Lystra, where the young Timothy joined him, and Troas (the ancient Troy) where Luke began to accompany Paul. On the return journey, Paul spent some time at Ephesus before returning to Caesarea, Jerusalem and finally Antioch. A selection of events and experiences — everything from healings to imprisonments — during this second journey are offered by Luke in Acts 16-18.

During this journey he stayed in Corinth for many months, establishing a church in that city. The year was about 50-51. During his labors in Corinth, Paul received word from Silas and Timothy, who had stayed in Thessalonica, that the Gospel was being proclaimed but there were some problems in the Church. Paul responded with two letters written during his Corinth residency (see 1 and 2 Thessalonians; some scholars argue that Paul only wrote 1 Thessalonians).

Paul made his way back to Antioch, his home base. Luke tells us that "after spending some time there he departed and went from place to place through the region of Galatia and Phrygia, strengthening all the disciples" (Acts 18:23). This begins his *third missionary* effort to the Gentiles. On this, his last official missionary journey, he again "strengthens" the converts and spends three years at Ephesus.

During his stay at Ephesus, Paul begins his letter-writing ministry to the churches he has established. Assuming Galatians and the Thessalonian letters as his only writings to new Christians thus far, he now launched into a series of epistles that comprise the majority of the New Testament.

While resident in Ephesus, Paul receives news that the Corinth Church is having difficulty. Paul first writes a letter (1 Corinthians) to help them with their problems. But learning that his letter was having no effect, Paul pays a brief visit to Corinth (2 Corinthians 1:1). Eventually Paul writes at least one further letter (some believe 2 Corinthians 10-13 is a third letter) during his stay at Ephesus.

Biblical scholars are divided over two other letters of Paul which may have been written during his stay in Ephesus. The first letter is the Epistle to the Church at Philippi. It is traditionally thought to have been written during Paul's imprisonment in Rome (60-63) while he was awaiting trial. Some have said it was written during an imprisonment in Ephesus.

A further possibility dating from this period is a letter we have already noted, that is, Galatians. Some have argued that Paul wrote his Letter to the Galatians during his stay at Ephesus. This debate centers around the territory designated by the name "Galatia." Is this letter directed to the people in the north of Asia Minor or the south? If it is written to the people of the north, then Paul would have written his Epistle to the Galatians from Ephesus about the year 54, because he did not visit this territory until his second missionary journey (about 49 to 52). If Paul was writing to the people in the south of Galatia, then he would have been writing earlier following his first missionary journey (about 46 to 49). Perhaps we will never know for sure which letter Paul wrote first.

Antioch was Paul's home base for his Gentile mission. This city was crucial for the spread of early Christianity. However, the most important city of the empire was Rome. Here was the center of the known world and a place of major importance for spreading the Gospel of Jesus Christ. This may have been part of Paul's thinking as he leaves Ephesus and travels to Corinth (Acts 20:2-3). While resident in Corinth, for about three months during the year 58, Paul writes his Letter to the Roman Church.

There had already been a flourishing Christian community there and Paul had plans to visit them. Perhaps Paul was concerned about the possible Judean influence that he had confronted in Antioch and thus wanted to clarify his understanding of the Gospel of Christ. Or perhaps Paul felt the Good News of the Gospel should be taken to other regions. Jesus did tell His disciples at His Ascension: "Go therefore and make disciples of all nations, baptizing them in the name of the Father and of the Son and of the Holy Spirit" (Matthew 28:19). Paul indicates to the Christians in Rome some further missionary intentions beyond the Mediterranean area. He writes, "I shall go on by way of you to Spain; and I know that when I come to you I shall come in the fullness of the blessing of Christ" (Romans 15:28-29). So Paul writes this letter as an introduction to himself and his understanding of the Gospel as he anticipates his visit to Rome. He states in the beginning, "I long to see you, that I may impart to you some spiritual gift to strengthen you . . . that we may be mutually encouraged by each other's faith" (Romans 1:11-12).

But first, Paul had to remember the poor in Jerusalem. He writes to the Christians in Rome: "At present . . . I am going to Jerusalem with aid for the saints. For Macedonia and Achaia have been pleased to make some contribution for the poor among the saints at Jerusalem; they were pleased to do it, and indeed they are in debt to them, for if the Gentiles have come to share in their spiritual blessings, they ought also to be of service to them in material blessings" (Romans 15:25-27; see also 1 Corinthians 16:1). Paul had been accused of rejecting the law as a means to salvation and was therefore considered a traitor to the Christian faith (Romans 15:32 and Acts 21:20-21). Here was Paul taking pains to make a contribution by way of Gentile converts (who were free from the law!) to the Jewish Church in Jerusalem. Paul is attempting to make a healing and reconciling gesture to his Jewish opponents for the sake of the Gospel and the unity of the Church.

Paul's trip to Jerusalem with the collected offering is the beginning of the events that lead to his martyrdom. This truly was a dangerous place for Paul to visit (see Acts 21:10ff). On the journey, he stopped to see the elders of the Church at Ephesus (Acts 20:17) and addressing them as if for the last time (Acts 20:25, 36-38), he said, "I do not account my life of any value nor as precious to myself, if only I may accomplish my course and the ministry which I received from the Lord Jesus, to testify to the gospel of the grace of God" (Acts 20:24). Paul wished to reach Jerusalem for the feast of Pentecost, in the spring of 58 (Acts 20:16 and 21:17).

In Jerusalem, James, the leader of the Church, explained the situation to Paul. Many Jews had come to believe and they remained keen to keep the Jewish law. But "they have been told about you that you teach all the Jews who are among the Gentiles to forsake Moses, telling them not to circumcise their children or observe the customs. What then is to be done?" (Acts 21:21-22). A plan is devised for Paul to purify himself along with four other men (Acts 21:23ff). This included a process of fasting and prayer which took seven days.

However, the plan backfired. Jews from Asia (Minor) where Paul had done his Gentile missionary work spotted him in the temple and excited the crowd. Paul was accused of teaching against the law and defiling the temple by bringing Greeks into the inner court (Acts 21:27-29). This second accusation was one of the few laws that the Romans allowed to carry the death penalty. In Paul's time, a sign over the main gate of the temple warned those who may be ignorant of the Jewish law. Written in three languages, the inscription recovered by archaeologists read: "No foreigner may enter within the barricade which surrounds the temple and its enclosure. Anyone who is caught doing so will have himself to blame for his ensuing death." A riot followed and the mob attempted to murder Paul, but he was rescued by the Roman commander (Acts 21:30-36).

Paul is imprisoned in Jerusalem after the Roman

commander learns he is a Roman citizen (Acts 22:22-29). He is then brought before the Sanhedrin, but his meeting ended in a quarrel when Paul perceived that some were Pharisees and others Sadducees. Because the Sadducees did not believe in the Resurrection and the Pharisees did, Paul addressed them thus: "Brethren, I am a Pharisee, a son of Pharisees; with respect to the hope and the resurrection of the dead I am on trial" (Acts 23:6). Individuals then began plotting the murder of Paul.

Paul was taken under strong guard to the Roman garrison at Caesarea on the coast of Palestine (Acts 23:12-24). Like Jesus, Paul was brought before the Roman procurator Felix for creating a civil disorder. Apparently thinking Paul innocent, he delayed his decision in the hope that time would heal the tension (Acts 24:1-26). Suddenly Felix is called to Rome (about 59) and the new procurator, Porcius Festus, hears Paul's case. Paul perhaps sensed the hopeless situation, and wanting to go to Rome anyway, exercises his civil rights in appealing to the emperor himself, the supreme court of the empire (Acts 25:1-12). Herod Agrippa II visited Caesarea and Paul was again heard (Acts 26:1-32). Finally Paul was sent to Rome accompanied by Luke and Aristarchus. They traveled on a "prison ship" of convicted criminals, individuals who were being sent to Rome to face death by way of gladiators or wild beasts — either method preferred to the slow death of crucifixion.

The account of this voyage to Rome (Acts 27-28:13) is still today considered a rare description of ancient sea travel. The voyage included storms and shipwrecks, and after traveling north of Cyprus and south of Crete over to Melita and Sicily, Paul arrives in Puteoli, just southwest of Neapolis (Acts 28:14ff). Paul had arrived at the place where God had told him to bear witness (Acts 23:11).

Paul is imprisoned in Rome, held under a type of

house arrest until his trial (Acts 28:16). After three days, Paul called together the local leaders and said, "Brethren, though I had done nothing against the people or the customs of our fathers, yet I was delivered prisoner from Jerusalem into the hands of the Romans" (Acts 28:17). Paul then addressed many Christians in Rome who gathered to hear him in his "house-cell." Luke concludes his narrative with these words: "He lived there two whole years at his own expense [paying his own rent], and welcomed all who came to him, preaching the kingdom of God and teaching about the Lord Jesus Christ quite openly and unhindered" (28:30-31).

During Paul's house arrest in Rome (either 60-62 or 61-63), he received word from some of the churches that problems were developing. Paul responds by writing (probably) four important letters, epistles to the churches at Colossae, Philippi and Ephesus and then a personal letter to Philemon who lived in the city of Colossae. In each of these letters he refers to himself as a prisoner. (However, many scholars argue that Paul did not write Ephesians and Colossians. Other scholars date Philemon and Philippians to the early 50s.)

Whether Paul wrote Titus and 1 and 2 Timothy (known as the pastoral epistles) is uncertain and depends upon the year of Paul's martyrdom. If Paul was freed and allowed to make a further journey to Asia Minor, then he probably authored these epistles. If he was martyred at the end of his imprisonment, then the letters would possibly have been written in Paul's name by his followers and disciples. Our two sources, Luke's Acts and Paul's Epistles, give no clear indication that Paul was able to make a further missionary journey either west or east. Scholars have difficulty in aligning the complex Church organization found in the pastoral epistles with Paul's earlier writings; doctrinal teachings are different, either lacking popular Pauline themes or introducing new themes; further, vocabulary and style are different in the pastorals when compared to Paul's earlier writings. Because of these uncertainties and our interest to deal with the "undisputed" letters of Paul (that is, letters written by Paul or directly influenced by Paul), we will leave these pastoral writings for another time.

The dating of Paul's death is very difficult indeed. It is not certain when he died, although Church tradition (the writings of early Christian leaders which are not always accurate about dates) suggests martyrdom in Rome under the persecutions of Nero, 64 to 68. Clement of Rome (bishop c. 100) states that Paul went on to Spain and then returned to Rome and was martyred. Eusebius, a Church historian from the early fourth century, writes: "There is evidence that, having then been brought to trial, the apostle again set out on the ministry of preaching, and having appeared a second time in the same city found fulfillment in his martyrdom" (*Ecclesiastical History*, 2.22). Nevertheless, it is generally accepted that Paul was martyred under Nero, but the exact year remains a mystery.

According to another Church leader (Dionysius of Corinth, c. 170), Paul and Peter were martyred at the same time and buried in Rome. Although Paul's remains were transferred to the catacombs on the Appian Way (the main southern "highway" approaching Rome) during the Valerian persecutions in the latter half of the third century, they were returned to their original burial place where Constantine built a basilica in the fourth century.

Such was the life of Paul the Apostle. In the end we know only a small amount of accurate historical knowledge about the person who so influenced and spearheaded the rapid growth and spread of Christianity. However, we do know something of his thinking and his understanding of the Christian faith. Two themes clearly stand out in Paul's life and — as we shall see — in his writings.

First of all, for Paul the living and resurrected Christ was a splendid and exciting reality. Here was the heart of the matter — the living person of Christ. Without Him there is no hope. As Paul wrote with wonderful enthusiasm to the Corinthian Christians, "If Christ has not been raised, then our preaching is in vain and your faith is in vain. . . . If for this life only we have hoped in Christ, we are of all men most to be pitied" (1 Corinthians 15:14, 19). Hence Paul truly was — and encouraged others to be — a person *"In Christ,"* the living and resurrected Lord (2 Corinthians 12:2). Because of this person at the center, Paul found and proclaimed true freedom, peace and life.

Second, it is worth noting that throughout the book of Acts, in the life of Paul and in the life of the early Church, the Holy Spirit is present. Through prayerful worship and holy conversations with the living Christ, the Spirit of the living God guides, beckons, directs and leads Paul and the other members of the early Church. One could hardly say, based on the life of Paul (and Christ!), that this means a trouble-free, secure and easy life. But there is a special peace that seems to come upon those who seek the will of God above all else in their lives. God's love for humanity is profound and Paul gives us an example for responding to that love. This is the substance and heart of the Christian faith.

Paul's Letters

Very briefly we must consider the structure and form of Paul's letters in order to enhance our study of their content.

It was normal for a person writing a letter in the Greco-Roman world of Paul's day to include four general parts. First came the *opening statement*, which was a sentence giving the name of the sender, the name of the addressee and a very brief greeting. Second came a *thank-you statement*, offering a gracious word of appreciation or thanks — still a popular way to begin a letter. Third came the *message statement* which was the basic purpose for writing the letter. Fourth came a *final greetings statement* which was simply a farewell.

Hence, for example, the Church Father Athanasius, Bishop of Alexandria, wrote in 340 this letter concerning the celebration of a church festival day:

> To the Beloved Brother, and our fellow Minister Serapion (*opening statement*):
>
> Thanks be to Divine Providence for those things which, at all times, it vouchsafes to us (*thank-you statement*);
>
> Having, therefore, according to custom, written the Letter respecting the festival, etc. (*message statement*)...
>
> Salute one another with a holy kiss. All the brethren who are with me salute you (*final greetings statement*).

Paul's letters clearly hold to this accepted and traditional form of writing letters. For example, to the Roman Christian community, whom he had not met when he penned his letter, he writes the following:
"Paul, a servant of Jesus Christ . . . to all God's beloved in Rome" (Romans 1:1, 7). "First, I thank my God through Jesus Christ for all of you. . ." (Romans 1:8). The theme of his message is stated in Romans 1:16:

"For I am not ashamed of the gospel: it is the power of God for salvation to every one who has faith. . . ." (Paul's *message* section usually carries a "doctrinal" and "ethical" exhortation.) Paul's final greetings are found in Romans 16:25-27 where he includes a final benediction. This general format can be found in all of Paul's letters.

Paul wrote these letters in response to concrete problems. His sole purpose was to proclaim the Good News of Jesus Christ and so build up the Church, the body of Christ. As he saw fit, he included varying types of material in order to communicate the Gospel. For example, he seems to have used bits of homilies (Romans 1:18-32), early Church hymns (Philippians 2:6-11; Romans 8:31-39; 1 Corinthians 13); ancient liturgical formulas (1 Corinthians 11:24-25; 12:3; 16:22) and even sayings of Jesus that are sometimes not found in the Gospels (1 Corinthians 7:10-11; 9:14; 11:23-24; 1 Thessalonians 4:16-17; see also Acts 20:35: "It is more blessed to give than to receive").

Based on our overview of Paul's life, it is clear that these letters are a substitute for his actual presence. When Paul could not travel to Corinth, or Galatia, or Philippi, or elsewhere, he sent a letter attempting to deal with the concrete problems the Christian converts were confronting. Certainly he would have preferred to be in their presence, so the communication became a second best. Hence he could write to the Romans, "I long to see you . . . I want you to know, brethren, that I have often intended to come to you (but thus far have been prevented) . . . so I am eager to preach the gospel to you also who are in Rome" (Romans 1:11, 13, 15). These "substitutes" for Paul's visits were probably regionally circulated among churches (see 2 Corinthians 10:10, for example). Probably within a decade of their composition, Paul's letters would have been collected as available and read aloud during their meetings and worship services as basic authoritative Christian writings for practical daily advice and instruction.

Finally, it was common in the first century to dictate letters. If you did not wish to write yourself, one could dictate word for word or dictate the message while trusting its formulation to a secretary. Paul apparently used both of these methods (although which dictation method he used is not known). Romans, for example, appears to have been dictated to Tertius: "I, Tertius, the writer of this letter, greet you in the Lord" (Romans 16:22). In his First Letter to the Church at Corinth, Paul apparently writes only the ending: "I, Paul, write this greeting with my own hand" (1 Corinthians 16:21; see also 2 Thessalonian 3:17 and Colossians 4:18). In his Letter to the Galatians, Paul seems to compare his handwriting with perhaps the writer of the letter: "See with what large letters I am writing to you with my own hand" (Galatians 6:11; see also Philemon 19).

Keeping these things in mind, that is, that the letters deal with concrete situations and are a substitute for his presence, Paul's letters have apostolic authority. They are instruments of spiritual guidance and direction. They attempt to deal with problems — apostolically and therefore authoritatively. The Spirit of God chose to work through them as instruments of grace long ago and so we at the least are about to travel where wonderful spiritual activity once occurred. It is to be hoped that if we go forward humbly and prayerfully, some new movings of the Spirit will stir and enliven our spirit as each of us — like Paul — travel "faithfully" in pursuit of our spiritual journey. Only in this manner will we find, to quote a favorite Pauline phrase, "peace from God our Father and the Lord Jesus Christ" (1 Corinthians 1:3; Romans 1:7; 2

Corinthians 1:2; Galatians 1:3; Ephesians 1:2; and others).

We will approach the letters of Paul with the following structure: each chapter will examine one of his epistles by considering (1) the historical context and situation the letter addresses; (2) a general summary of content; (3) selected passages for everyday Christian living.

CHAPTER TWO

Paul's Letter
to the Romans

It is generally accepted that Paul wrote his Letter to the
Churches in Rome about the year 57 or 58. Toward the
end of Paul's third missionary journey and while resident
in Corinth, Paul writes to the Christians in Rome telling
them he is "satisfied . . . that you yourselves are full of
goodness" (Romans 15:14) and telling them of his plans:
"I hope to see you in passing as I go to Spain, and to be
sped on my journey there by you, once I have enjoyed
your company for a little. At present, however, I am
going to Jerusalem with aid for the saints" (Romans
15:24-25).

Paul had never met the Christians in Rome but must
have been painfully aware of their importance. There
could be no satisfactory spreading of the Good News of
the Gospel without including the main city of the empire.
So why not include a stay over in this vital city during his
evangelization of the western edge of the empire? As
Paul himself states, the Holy Spirit made his "ambition
to preach the gospel, not where Christ has already been
named, lest I build on another man's foundation" (Romans 15:20).

This is Paul's longest letter written as an advance
explanation of his Gospel. Its purpose is to prepare the

Christians in Rome for his planned brief visit as he launches a further missionary journey. Perhaps Paul sensed through the Holy Spirit his pending visit to Rome (15:29), but at the time of writing his epistle he was unaware of the circumstances that would eventually bring him to the imperial city. Yet Paul was aware that trouble could await him in Jerusalem. Rather anxiously he writes to the Christians in Rome, "I appeal to you, brethren . . . to strive together with me in your prayers to God on my behalf, that I may be delivered from the unbelievers in Judea . . . so that by God's will I may come to you with joy and be refreshed in your company" (Romans 15:30-32).

Historical Context

It is not known when the Roman Churches were founded or who was instrumental in their beginnings. A burial inscription dated A.D. 43 (for Pomponia Graecina) indicates she was a Christian. This would indicate a very early date for the coming of Christianity to Rome, perhaps less than a decade after the death and resurrection of Christ. Paul mentions that he had wanted to visit the Roman Churches for many years (Romans 15:23).

The background of the young Christian community was not free from problems. Suetonius, a Roman biographer who penned *The Lives of the Twelve Caesars* (early second century), indicates there was tension in the Jewish community. He writes that in the year A.D. 49, Emperor Claudius "expelled from Rome the Jews who were constantly stirring up a tumult under the leadership of Christus [Christ]." This rather severe punishment resulted in Paul meeting Aquila and Priscilla in Corinth, who had "lately come from Italy . . . because Claudius had commanded all the Jews to leave Rome" (Acts

18:1-2). Not only does this indicate that Paul had some firsthand knowledge of the Christians in Rome but also that there was tension in Rome between Jewish Christians and Gentile Christians. These two resources must have had some influence on Paul as he prepared to write his Epistle to Rome.

After the death of Claudius, in the year 54, the Jewish community was allowed to return to the city. Three or four years later, when Paul begins his letter, the old tension between the Jewish Christians and Gentile Christians is probably well underway and Paul seems aware of the difficulties. Although Paul lacks exact knowledge of the circumstances and the people in Rome, he addresses the concrete issues — issues that he has become familiar with during his ministry to the Gentiles (Romans 11:13).

The issues seem to be twofold and very contemporary. On the one hand, the Gentile Christians apparently emphasized justification by God's grace. However, this essential belief caused some problems for the Jewish Christians. If one relied upon the grace of God alone, then what about the ancient God-ordained traditions of the Jewish faith? Does this mean the Jewish law is worthless? Were dietary laws practiced by Jewish converts of no value? Has the Church made redundant the nation of Israel? The Jewish Christians must have concluded that it was better to keep the ancient Jewish traditions of Torah (or law) and eating habits than allow immorality and lawlessness to rule the Church. Perhaps their objections were well-founded because of the questionable morality of some Gentile Roman Christians. Perhaps the received ethical code of the Roman Empire was accepted as compatible with justification by the grace of God — and was certainly preferable to the Jewish law code.

Hence Paul was to deal with Jewish Christian objections. He states their questions without ducking the issue: "Are we to continue in sin that grace may abound?" (Romans 6:1); "Are we to sin because we are not under law but under grace?" (Romans 6:15). Have God's promises to His chosen people failed? (See Romans 9:6.) Many Jewish converts during this early period of the Christian faith would have attended both the synagogue and the Christian community, seeing no conflict. But as the tension grew and the non-Christian Jews questioned the compatibility of the "two" faiths, God commissioned Paul to assist in the controversy.

On the other hand, the attitude of the Gentile Christians to the Jewish Christians was strained. The Gentile community resented the pressure to become a proselyte Jew in order to become a Christian. They were attracted to the message of God's grace in Jesus Christ, but they did not wish to first become a part of the Jewish religion. They wanted to be under grace and not the law (Romans 6:15). So Paul, aware of this two-directional issue, and being in a unique position to deal with it, writes his letter to the troubled Christian community in Rome with hope of reconciling the tension and preparing for his pending visit.

Summary of Contents

After a lovely salutation and thanksgiving statement (Romans 1:1-17), Paul argues that neither the Jews nor the Gentiles were able to do God's will. Although the Jews had an advantage (Romans 3:1-8), all are guilty, both Jew and Gentile (Romans 3:9-20). So God sent His Son, Jesus Christ, because all have sinned and are in need of God's grace (Romans 3:23-26). Now all boasting is excluded (Romans 3:27-31).

Abraham is justified by faith, and the true descendants of Abraham are all who have faith in Jesus Christ, both Jew and Gentile (Romans 4). Paul then discussed the consequences of justification as the answer to the Adam and Christ analogy: through one person came sin and through one person comes justification (Romans 5).

Paul employs three images to speak of the new age in Christ. He uses the image of *baptism* to ask how anyone could share in the new life and still live in the old ways (Romans 6). Then he uses the image of *slavery* to show that a person in the grace of God is no longer a slave to sin but to God (Romans 6). Next Paul employs the image of *marriage* stating that a woman is not bound to her deceased husband and so no person in the grace of God is bound to sin.

Then Paul turns to the explanation of his mission to the Gentiles (Romans 9-11). Here he attempts to work through all the objections that the Jewish Christians would raise to his Gentile mission and to Gentiles in general. Has God turned away from Israel toward the Gentiles? Has God abandoned His promises to Israel? Why has not God made the hearts of the Jews receptive to Jesus? Are Jews excluded from salvation? Is God a just God? Paul assures the Jewish Christians that God has not forsaken His promises and the Gentiles and Israel will in the end receive His mercy.

In a profound section, Paul speaks of the consecrated life of the Christian (Romans 12-13). Christians have clear responsibilities, called upon to practice the law of love and respect the state. He then speaks of Christ's imminent second coming (Romans 13:11-14). Before ending with personal notes (chapter 15) and general greetings (chapter 16), Paul again writes of love and respect of others encouraging the strong to help the weak (Romans 14).

Passages for Everyday Living

> *Paul, a servant [or slave] of Jesus*
> *Christ, called to be an apostle, set apart*
> *for the gospel of God . . . the gospel con-*
> *cerning his Son . . . designated Son of God*
> *in power according to the Spirit of holiness*
> *by his resurrection from the dead . . .*
> *through whom we have received grace*
> *and apostleship. . . . To all God's beloved*
> *in Rome . . . called to be saints . . . I men-*
> *tion you always in my prayers (Romans*
> *1:1-9).*

Paul's first thoughts are clearly stated to the Roman Christians, fellow believers whom he has yet to meet. He refers to himself as a "slave" and by identifying his Gospel of the "resurrected" Son of God. His immediate goal is to put the Roman Churches at ease concerning these key issues, that is, himself and the Gospel. As a fruit of this effort, we capture a clear indication of how Paul understands the Christian faith.

Paul refers to himself as a servant or "slave" of his Lord. This term applies to all Christians and to the Church, the body of Christ. Paul uses this term thirty times to refer to himself as one who reflects the work of his Master. To the Philippians Paul writes that he "emptied himself, taking the form of a servant" (Philippians 2:7). The work of his master freed *all* Christians from sin (Romans 6:18); now a new and living communion can be experienced. Believers are the body of Christ who have been forced for a relationship with the living God. As God was free to love in Christ, so we are now free to love God in Christ.

Paul finds himself called to be an Apostle. Each Christian believer has a particular calling or vocation that is "assigned" to him or her in the kingdom of God. No one is without a "ministry." No sincere follower of the Master is without orders. No one lives in a manner that would free him or her from responsibility. On the other hand, everyone's realm of influence is unique and without duplication. No one is called to be a "slave" in the same way as another. No one is set apart for the same task. Like Jesus Christ, we are called to be trustworthy servants of God the Father.

Paul's Gospel is that of Christ resurrected. He is not a servant or slave by force. He is not chained to his task. Rather he is free from sin — sin which obstructs and distances one from God the creator. But now sin has been overcome because the cycle of sin and death has been broken. He lives! He has cut through the debris. Those who believe in Him can live too, in right relationship with God for eternity. This is the essence of the Gospel of Jesus Christ, and Paul wants to make sure that the Roman Christians understand the message he preaches.

Paul then refers to the believers in Rome as "saints." In the Old Testament, anything that comes into contact with God is considered holy. Hence garments, vessels, places, the temple, are considered holy because of contact with God. This is the basic sense the word has throughout the history of Christianity. Paul then is referring to the Roman believers as those who are in contact and in "proper touch" with God. When one is in *right relationship* with the living God, they reflect the very holiness of God such as St. Augustine, Gregory of Nyssa, Julian of Norwich, St. Francis of Assisi, and others.

Paul's right relationship with God is reflected in the end of our passage. He states that the believers in Rome are in his prayers. He is constantly ("without ceasing," Romans 1:9) in conversation with the Father through Christ and in the Holy Spirit. He wants to come visit them (Romans 1:10) and sees them as part of his spiritual responsibility. For Paul, a true and healthy relationship with the living God through the resurrected Christ requires constant and continual conversation and communion.

* * *

> *For I am not ashamed of the gospel: it is the power of God for salvation to every one who has faith. . . . For in it the righteousness of God is revealed through faith for faith. . . (Romans 1:16-17).*

Paul begins to expand his understanding of the Gospel. Here is stated the theme of the entire epistle: the revealing of God's righteousness. The missionary experience for Paul has clearly proven the saving power of God for those who believe.

God's righteousness is a key phrase. For Paul, it probably had some moral overtones but more importantly and in the Hebrew sense, it carried the meaning of *activity*. God is acting within the arena of human experience. It has been argued that the Church could not have developed historically without continual activity from God. This was certainly true for Paul as he witnessed time and again God acting in the midst of his missionary work. Many times the ways of God are seen as mysterious — a favorite word of the early Church Fathers. But here Paul indicates that God reveals His ways on occasion which can be clear, exciting and even overwhelming.

The age of righteousness, according to the Old Testament prophets (see especially Isaiah 51, 55 and Jeremiah 31), was some time in the future. For Paul (the onetime Pharisee), the future age that was to come had arrived. Paul's use of the present tense Greek verb is critical:

God's righteousness *is being revealed now*! Paul later indicates that this revelation is not yet completed, but "D-Day" or "the landing" has happened in the person Jesus Christ.

More exactly, and in light of Paul's missionary experience, history is fulfilled. Evil has been defeated by the life, death, resurrection and ascension of Christ. This is the power of the Gospel. Paul is not emphasizing a mere message or philosophy of life. God's power has been shown. The creation and continual inspiration of the Church through the Holy Spirit is clearly an ongoing righteous act of God's revelation.

Paul's use of the word "faith" indicates the terms of God's revelation. God's "revealing" righteousness is a matter of faith from beginning to end. As Paul indicates in his Epistle to the Galatians (3:11ff; also compare Romans 4), faith can be contrasted with merit gained by keeping the law (exemplified in Abraham). If we can fulfill the law in perfect obedience, then one can be saved through the law. We cannot. Hence like Abraham (who lived *before* the law), live like Abraham by faith. God is trustworthy (1 Corinthians 1:9 and 10:13; 1 Thessalonians 5:24).

Faith then is an attitude in which we recognize our own insufficiency for life (in the ultimate face of evil and death). So we must rely upon the sufficiency of God. We do not earn merits by keeping the law — this is misplaced faith ultimately directed to the self. Like Abraham we must trust God. So faith, like God's righteousness, is an *act*.

St. Anselm, a twelfth-century Church Father, wrote that "faith leads to understanding." He seems to be echoing Paul's statement to the believers in Rome, "God is revealed through faith for faith" (Romans 1:17). Through faith we apprehend a portion of God's truth reaffirming faith in the living, acting God. Faith leads to deeper faith — this is true for every use of faith regardless of subject matter. One must begin any undertaking with some "faith."

This then is the power of God. He acts on our behalf putting us right with himself. Hence, in the Gospel, Paul is not ashamed to proclaim that faith is the clue to real life — it is the door to salvation. The Greek word *salvatio* means "to deliver" or preserve one from grave danger (see Acts 7:25 and 27:34, for example). In the midst of all the uncertainties Paul had to face proclaiming the Gospel, including the anger of his own Jewish people and rejection by the Gentile community, Paul could not be ashamed of his Gospel even in the cosmopolitan capitol city of Rome. Why? Because his trust was in the Christ who lives mediating a right relationship between God and humanity.

* * *

> *... all have sinned and fall short of the glory of God, they are justified by his grace as a gift, through the redemption which is in Christ Jesus (Romans 3:23-24).*

Paul is aware that both Jew and Gentile make up the Christian community in Rome. Yet neither has an advantage. This entire section of the epistle (Romans 1:16; 4:25) expands his beginning assertions that through the Gospel, God's righteousness justifies those who believe. Without this Gospel, all humanity stands condemned, unacceptable before God — "all have sinned." Whether male or female, white or black, Jew or Greek, all stand in need of being put in right relationship with the Creator.

What does Paul mean by the "glory of God"? God is the eternal being who is controlled by nothing. This is His wonder and glory — His permanence, perfection and constancy. These are the very characteristics humanity longs to possess. Ironically, these characteristics can only be received through a proper, wholistic and right relationship with God. But all have sinned, all have turned in another direction seeking these very characteristics, seeking to be like God. So we all fall short of glorifying God with our lives. We live for self rather than for God. As a result, we lack wholeness, peace of mind and a right place in the ongoing flow of life, that is, the place of worship to God from within life's circumstances.

So God gives us His *grace as a gift*. This grace gift is precisely Jesus Christ. His life was lived, says Paul, on our behalf because we have sinned and fallen short. As Augustine says, Christ picked us up from the gutter of life and healed our wounds by His own sacrifice, nursing us back to health (so Augustine interprets the parable of the Good Samaritan, Luke 10:25-37). Now we can have a full and potentially complete relationship with Him whom we were meant to worship, God the Father. This is all a *gift*! This is "amazing grace" that does not have to be earned, only accepted.

Hence we are freely *justified*. In effect, we are put right with God. All the charges against us in a law-court sense have been dropped. Rebellious humanity that we are, we prodigal sons and daughters are acquitted of any wrongdoing and welcomed home with a holy kiss (see the lovely parable dealing with this theme in Luke 15:11-32, "the lost son"). We are now delivered from oppression, persecution, imprisonment and punishment. The incredible truth of the Gospel is that we do not receive what we deserve. We have earned God's hatred, and instead are given His love! In this way, human guilt before

God — a universal human sense — is replaced by thankfulness and worship. In every form of human religion, there is an offering of "justification," an attempt to deal with that sixth sense of the human situation telling of an alienation and forlornness existing between the creature and the universe, or more explicitly the creature and the Creator.

This is exemplified in the way Jesus preached and taught. He did not go to those who were healthy but those who were in need of a physician (Mark 2:17). Luke tells of how "the tax collectors and sinners were all drawing near to him. And the Pharisees and the scribes murmured, saying, 'This man receives sinners and eats with them' " (Luke 15:1-2). Again, Jesus tells the story of the lost sheep and how the shepherd (God) is greatly concerned and seeks after those who lack ability to find Him (Matthew 18:12-14). God comes after us and acts in our favor, justifying us with the free gift of grace, that is, Jesus Christ.

* * *

> But God shows his love for us in that
> while we were yet sinners Christ died for
> us (Romans 5:8).

This verse combines two monumental truths: God's love for us and Christ's death for us. For Paul, these two truths are not in contradiction. There is no question of how mercy and justice can be understood. God is God and Christ Jesus has loved us with the perfect love that gave himself for humanity.

Within a few decades of Christ's death and resurrection, the Church began to develop a vocabulary for speaking of God's self-giving love for humanity. One of the key words, if not *the* key word, in this vocabulary is the

Greek term *agapē* (that is, the particular Christian word for love). In the environment of that day, it was assumed by pagans that gods did not love mortals. Even for Aristotle, God can have no object of love outside of himself. In this context Paul's statement is amazing. To suggest that love is the very nature of God, that is, love toward us His creatures, is a radical break with pagan thought introducing the unprecedented word agape for the Christian view of God. It is little wonder that Christianity was attractive to the pagan world.

It follows then that if agape is the love of God toward humanity, the redeemed should reflect that love in daily life. This basic Christian term stands for something essentially Christian. It designates God's love for Christ His Son and for all humanity, and Christ's love for humanity. But at the same time it is a peculiar Christian affection designating humanity's loving response to God's love and the reflection of that love to fellow humans — in particular those who are in the world of our daily living.

Peter once asked Jesus, "How often shall my brother sin against me, and I forgive him?" (Matthew 18:21-22). Jesus responded, "Seventy times seven." (There is no limit, seven being a number in Judaism of divine significance.) Then Jesus tells Peter and the other disciples the parable about the king and a servant who did not carry the king's forgiveness into the marketplace of life (Matthew 18:23-35). Or who can ignore Jesus' penetrating words, "As you did it to one of the least of these my brethren, you did it to me" (Matthew 25:40)? This statement is surrounded by Jesus' thrice-stated command to feed the hungry, give drink to the thirsty, welcome the stranger, clothe the naked and visit the sick and imprisoned. How can the agape of God, that loved us while we were yet sinners, not be shared with those whom we meet daily along life's way?

* * *

*The death he [Christ] died he died to
sin, once for all, but the life he lives he
lives to God. So you also must consider
yourselves dead to sin and alive to God in
Christ Jesus (Romans 6:10-11).*

Now we are free from self and free for God. This is
accomplished through union with Christ Jesus. But there
appears to be a difficulty here: if salvation is an un-
deserved gracious gift of God, is sin literally encouraged? "Are we to sin because we are not under the law
but under grace?" (Romans 6:15). "By no means!" says
Paul. "Thanks be to God . . . you . . . have become slaves
of righteousness . . . for sanctification" (Romans
6:15-19). The reason for this is that Christ died to sin for
us from within our ranks.

Throughout this sixth chapter, sin is personified. Humanity is bound in servitude to sin because we are in the
"flesh." Christ through the incarnation became flesh, sin
put in its claim (through temptations) but he did not
yield. He lived in perfect obedience to God, even so far as
to die (Philippians 2:8). He died rather than sin! Sin's
power — as a "person" claiming rights — was denied and
so defeated. He died to sin, a death we can share in because He died as one of us. He literally condemned sin in
the flesh (Romans 8:3).

How do we share this victory? Paul concludes that by
being baptized into the Body of Christ we share in His
death and resurrection. Hence we are free from sin
(verse 7): because we died with Him and live with Him
(verse 8), we too shall never die (verse 9). We shall
"transfer" existence and be like the resurrected One
when our earthly life is finished, but death no longer is to
be feared because *He lives.*

So the "possible" difficulty is not real! Sin does not abound due to the free gift of grace because we are not just free — but free for God through our union with Christ in the Holy Spirit. Hence Paul indicates that we can now "live to God" because of our death to sin and being alive to Christ. But what does "live to God" mean for Paul?

As previously noted, he uses the word sanctification. This term, like agape, appears to be a somewhat unique Christian word. The Greek literally means "spiritual renewing." Paul deals with this term rather fully in the twelfth chapter of Romans where he speaks of transforming the mind (verse 2) and a new birth in the sense of a second stage in the salvation process. This is accomplished by the continual and subsequent renewing process of the Holy Spirit. This is the unceasing excitement, movement and growing *process* of the Christian life. How can sin abound in the practice of such freedom for God? Paul concludes: "For the wages of sin is death, but the free gift of God is eternal life in Christ Jesus our Lord" (Romans 6:23).

* * *

> *But you are not in the flesh, you are in the Spirit, if the Spirit of God really dwells in you. Any one who does not have the Spirit of Christ does not belong to him. . . . All who are led by the Spirit of God are sons of God . . . you have received the spirit of sonship. When we cry, "Abba! Father!" it is the Spirit himself bearing witness with our spirit that we are children of God (Romans 8:9-16).*

Accepting all that Paul has written to this point, he now interprets its meaning. This eighth chapter of Romans is equal in profundity, eloquence and stature to 1

Corinthians 13. Paul holds nothing back, pushing the significance of his previous statements to their logical conclusion.

Paul was no stranger to the workings of the Holy Spirit. The Spirit sent Paul on his missionary journeys (Acts 13:2, 4; see also Acts 6:1-6) and through Christ and the Holy Spirit he received his apostleship (Galatians 1:1). Also, Paul would have been well aware of the Spirit's importance in the Old Testament (see the stories, for example, surrounding Saul, Samson, Elijah, Elisha, Micah, and the prophecies of such individuals as Ezekiel and Zechariah). So it is not surprising that in Romans he uses the term "spirit" over twenty times in chapter 8 (and only five previous times in the epistle). The Holy Spirit is the key force in the second stage of the salvation process, Christ being the initiator, or first-stage protagonist.

For Paul, the Spirit of God is a tremendous power. This "Spirit" breaks into human lives directing Christians in the proper use of their new freedom in Christ. The believers are not left on their own to work things out the best they can. Among the early Christians, this seems to have been an overwhelming truth (see Acts 2:4). The work of the Holy Spirit was the proof of the age inaugurated by the resurrection of Christ.

Paul was certainly aware of the "abnormal manifestations" of the Spirit (speaking in tongues, healings). But he seemed more aware of the gifts of the Spirit beneath these manifestations. These deeper gifts were more enduring, real and constructive for the Church. They comprise the "more excellent way" (1 Corinthians 12:31), and can be summarized as "faith, hope, love . . . but the greatest of these is love" (1 Corinthians 13:13; compare Romans 8:5). This bottom-line term — love — is the supernatural element in Christian lives. It can be tested quite easily by simply looking for the love of Christ reflected in people's everyday living.

Paul's unrelenting conclusion is that if you do not possess the Spirit of Christ you do not belong to Him. It follows then that if you belong to Christ, the Spirit comes too. The New Testament is consistent in its witness that when one comes to Christ that person receives a supernatural gift of divine power. This was the early Church's general experience. We can be assured that the gift is there — all one has to do is make use of it.

As a result, believers are not just acquaintances of God, but His *children*. Now one can literally call God "Father" or "Daddy." Here is a further term that is uniquely appropriated by the early Church and given new and profound meaning. In Jesus' dramatic prayer at Gethsemane (Mark 14:36), He intimately addresses God as "Father." Now Paul, following the teachings and example of Jesus (Luke 11:1-4 and Matthew 6:9-13), reassures the Roman Christians that they are children of God. Hence "the Spirit helps us in our weakness; for we do not know how to pray as we ought, but the Spirit himself intercedes for us with sighs too deep for words" (Romans 8:26; also verse 27). The Spirit within is our *helper*. Such is the battle of the flesh. But because of our adoption, we become children and heirs of God. The Spirit of God does not leave us alone in the darkness of this world, but carefully and efficiently ushers God's children constantly into the light.

However, there are those who may choose not to be guided by the Spirit of God. These individuals are not children of God (Matthew 5:45). They decide to go another direction and forsake their "divine heritage." Throughout the biblical writings, as Paul continually emphasizes, God *created* humanity in His image so that the natural, true and only *relation* of creature to God is one of *dependence* and worship. As Augustine states in *City of God*, our happiness depends on God:

> *Although, therefore, they are not the supreme good, for God is a greater good, yet those mutable things which can adhere to the immutable good, and so be blessed, are very good; for so completely is He their good, that without Him they cannot but be wretched (12:1).*

We creatures of God can find no rest, peace or eternity save in a correct and living relationship with the Creator. Other goals may seem satisfying and appear more attractive, but in the end they will prove empty and valueless.

* * *

> *I consider that the sufferings of this present time are not worth comparing with the glory that is to be revealed to us. For the creation waits with eager longing for the revealing of the sons of God (Romans 8:18-19).*

Now Paul's assertions reach a final level. After his philosophical (chápters 1-3), biblical (chapters 4-6), psychological (chapter 7) and theological (chapter 8) arguments, he now becomes poetic in envisioning the future.

We live in the midst of problems. There is suffering and sickness and sorrow on all sides. The Christian is not immune from this sad state of affairs and so we too "groan inwardly" even though we have the first fruits of the Spirit (Romans 8:23). We groan or sigh because we sense our incompleteness, and hence lack satisfaction.

The whole of creation or nature "has been groaning in travail" (Romans 8:22). But for Paul, the clue to understanding all this pain, suffering and travail is in the spiritual life of humanity. We now have a foretaste of what is to come. In principle, we are children of the Father. Soon — and in the completeness of our bodies (as indicated in the resurrected Christ) — we shall in full actuality be the children of God (1 John 3:2; see also Romans 8:11; 2 Corinthians 5:1-8). This is our hope that is constantly experienced in the flow of God's love through the unwaverng power of the Holy Spirit. Hence it is a hope continually renewed as a pledge and foretaste of the future — it is something that *abides* (1 Corinthians 13:13; 2 Corinthians 4:18; 5:7). ". . . If we hope for what we do not see, we wait for it with patience" (Romans 8:25).

* * *

We know that in everything God works for good with those who love him, who are called according to his purpose. For those whom he foreknew he also predestined [or elected by grace] to be conformed to the image of his Son, in order that he might be the first-born among many brethren. And those whom he predestined he also called; and those whom he called he also justified; and those whom he justified he also glorified. What then shall we say to this? If God is for us, who is against us? (Romans 8:28-31).

Here Paul offers some of the most reassuring statements found in all of Scripture. The literal translation of verse 28 offers even more comfort and direct confidence in the God of the universe: "We know also that those who love God, called according to His purpose, He cooperates with aid and interest for good in every way." Paul is not arguing that everything is all right and will work out in the end. Rather, his emphasis is that *nothing* can separate us from the love of God (verse 35). God will cooperate with us and will work with us regardless of how desperate the situation. There is no possible situation in which God cannot be found. Now, through the reconciling work of Christ, we are united to the Father in such a way that nothing can develop where God's aid and interest are not present.

Life will not be troubleproof and without difficulty. Paul was certainly aware that troubles would present themselves. To the Christians at Corinth he writes "boasting" of his imprisonments, beatings, stonings, shipwrecks, lack of food and lodgings; "a night and a day I have been adrift at sea; on frequent journeys, in danger from rivers, danger from robbers, danger from my own people, danger from Gentiles, danger in the city, danger in the wilderness, danger at sea, danger from false brethren" (2 Corinthians 11:25-29). To be sure, Paul knew of the troubles and difficulties in life. Yet Paul rejoiced because God cooperates, aids and assists us in times of trial. God's grace was sufficient for Paul during life's strains and stresses and therefore His grace will be sufficient for the Christians in Rome whatever their trials.

God cooperates with those who have been called according to His purpose. Our love for God is not the determining factor, but everything is dependent upon God's love for us. We are called by His love spoken and acted in Christ. So we read in a later New Testament epistle, "In this is love, not that we loved God but that he loved us and sent his Son. . . ." (1 John 4:10; see also verse 19, "We love because he first loved us. . .). Hence, for Paul we are called according to His purpose and plan, that we be "the firstborn among many brethren."

71

It follows that salvation is a gift of God. It is not based upon what we do — for we cannot merit God's gift for justification. Our hope of salvation is entirely outside of ourselves. It is based upon the works of Jesus Christ, God's love toward us while we were yet rebellious. Now we are glorified through Christ in the Holy Spirit. So Paul asks, what can be concluded: "If God is for us, who is against us?" God now has an invested interest in humanity, His incarnate Son. From within God's purpose, we do not live without His aid, concern and constant interest. This, according to Paul, is the Christian's *wonderful assurance.*

* * *

Who shall separate us from the love of Christ? Shall tribulation, or distress, or persecution, or famine, or nakedness, or peril, or sword? . . . In all these things we are more than conquerers through him who loved us . . . neither death, nor life, nor angels, nor principalities, nor things present, nor things to come, nor powers, nor height, nor depth, nor anything else in all creation, will be able to separate us from the love of God in Christ Jesus our Lord (Romans 8:35-39).

Everything in the world seems radically against the truly committed Christian. But for Paul, as proven in his own life, anything that threatens a Christian's ultimate person will be soundly defeated. This has already happened in the person Jesus, who defeated the powers of darkness that threatened Him and now threatened His followers from all sides. He died and was resurrected and now pleads our case before the Father. What on "earth" could now threaten?

Sin cannot destroy our ultimate person (Romans 8:33). As we struggle to eliminate the sinful actions of our being (Romans 8:13), God perceives *only* what we are becoming in Christ through the Holy Spirit and we are acquitted. The judge *becomes* the attorney for our defense.

Then Paul lists several other types of calamities. Emotional distress, rejection by others, disease of body or mind, lack of bodily needs, even the sword (perhaps anticipating his own trip to Jerusalem) can certainly cause "feelings" of distance from God. They can make us unable to sense the love and assurance of God. But we must not trust our *feelings*. (See Jesus' rejection of feelings in the parable of the publican and Pharisee, Luke 18:9-14.) Christians are the called according to His purpose, hence even though troubles and difficulties may indicate God is distant, Paul says our concentration should be on the death and resurrection of Jesus Christ. Feelings do not justify us, Christ does. Feelings are not the essence of a relationship — although they play a part: love in action is the essence.

Next Paul goes on to mention even greater obstacles that bear upon all Christians: life and death, the present and the future, things up and down, things spiritual and physical. These are the mysteries of a world that is not completely known by Paul and by our modern scientific age. But Paul's certainty is complete simply because he does not concentrate on these distractions of life, but rather he subjects them all to the person of the resurrected Christ. Because he lives, God's aid and interest secures our person for eternity. We are beyond threat and can never be annihilated or extinguished. Or to say it in Paul's words: "Nothing can separate us from the love and life of God in Christ Jesus our Lord." (Reread Romans 1:17.)

* * *

> *I appeal to you therefore, brethren, by*
> *the mercies of God, to present your bodies*
> *as a living sacrifice, holy and acceptable*
> *to God, which is your spiritual worship.*
> *Do not be conformed to this world but be*
> *transformed by the renewal of your mind,*
> *that you may prove what is the will of*
> *God, what is good and acceptable and per-*
> *fect (Romans 12:1-2).*

After fully explaining God's purpose in history (chapters 9-11), Paul turns to the manner in which Christians reflect God's goodness and love. Paul has dealt with the theological issues and now he can turn to their practical application. Living in the Spirit of God, and in the midst of a new order, how should a person live? For Paul (and with Jesus), the Christian ethic must follow Christian belief, that is, faith leads to action.

This is the *spiritual harvest*. It occurs with the reaction of our spirit to God's Spirit from within life's circumstances. Regardless of one's station or setting in life, one is called (or predestined, elected) to participate in *the* spiritual harvest. Paul could not have known the exact circumstances for each Christian in Rome, but he could offer general guidelines for moral *quality* and character.

In this section of Romans (12:1-9) Paul writes of basic attitudes. The Christian's life is a thankful response to the mercy of God; that is, God has done for us what we could not do for ourselves. This grateful response is the essential beginning attitude of every Christian. The Christian is called to be a saint (1:7), called to belong to Christ (1:6 and 1 Corinthians 3:23) and is equipped with the Holy Spirit. The "call to holiness" for

Paul is not a human perfection detached from the perfection of God. Rather it is a holiness based upon and understood by the holiness and righteousness of God as made known in Jesus Christ.

The new spiritual harvest is the attitude of sacrifice. In all religions, sacrifice has a preeminent place. The Judaism of Paul's day, and familiar to some Roman Christians, accepted sacrifice as the central act of worship and ritual. This sacrifice acknowledged the holiness of God.

Now for Christian worshipers, Paul writes that the attitude of sacrifice emulates the holiness of God. The liturgy of worship in the early Church (the Greek word *leitourgia* literally means a public work) centered around the sacrificial death of Christ on the cross (see 1 Corinthians 11:23-26). This must have been a very powerful force in shaping the attitude of the "body of Christ." The believers of Christ's body understood their lives as living sacrifices — lives of obedience to God in every part of life and even unto death. However, it is always the sacrifice of Christ that grounds such an attitude in reality making it rational and a necessary response to God the Father.

This self-dedication response opens up a whole new life for the believer. Instead of being molded by this world the Christian is transformed and remade mentally or one's attitude is revolutionized. This suggests independent moral decision-making and insight. Christians are not transformed to become robots — or even mechanical angels. They are transformed to exercise freely and anew their worshipful (liturgical) everyday sacrificial response to God. After all, believers are now heirs and adopted children. This "new family" should recognize and seek the will of the Father, that is, what is good and acceptable for all concerned in God's creation.

75

This basic sacrificial attitude affects the whole congregation of believers. As Paul states, "Having gifts that differ according to the grace given to us, let us use them" (Romans 12:6). The gifts are for serving the congregation, but the danger is that they will make one complacent and self-satisfied. So Paul cautions: Think soberly and do not be an individualist. Think of yourself as a part of the whole congregation or holy society, the body of Christ (Romans 12:4-5). Each has been given a "measure of faith which God has assigned" (verse 3) and as we respond to God with this faith, the better we will understand God *and* ourselves. This will give us a sober estimate of ourselves and our gifts.

As Paul enumerates the various gifts (verses 6-8), he presents a group of believers having balanced unity. The key factor for the balance and the unity, as with understanding holiness and sacrifice, is the person Jesus Christ. He is the head of the body and all have their gifts because they are in living *relationship* with Him.

* * *

Let love be genuine; hate what is evil, hold fast to what is good; love one another with brotherly affection; outdo one another in showing honor. Never flag in zeal, be aglow with the Spirit, serve the Lord. Rejoice in your hope, be patient in tribulation, be constant in prayer. . . . Contribute to the needs of the saints, practice hospitality. . . . Live in harmony with one another. . . . If possible, so far as it depends upon you, live peaceably with all. . . . Do not be overcome by evil, but overcome evil with good (Romans 12:9-21).

In Paul's First Letter to the Corinthians, the gifts of the Spirit culminate in the greatest gift of all: charity, or love. In the Greek language, as noted above, the word is agape. The English translation of love is inadequate. This word is the sum of Christian duty for Paul. What does he mean by this term?

As in the other areas of sacrifice, redemption and others, Paul thinks from God to humanity. He understands agape (love) as primarily the action of God's nature (Romans 5:8). Because God acts first (as with Israel and the Old Testament), we can experience the divine love. Paul writes to Ephesus that we can "know the love of Christ which surpasses knowledge, that you may be filled with all the fulness of God" (Ephesians 3:19). What a wonderful thought! Knowledge cannot grasp the agape of God, only Christian *experience*. Hence it is difficult to speak of agape in "understandable" terminology, but we can be sure that the experience of God's redeeming love energizes us to live a life *reflecting* that love (Romans 5:5; 1 Corinthians 12:31-13:1).

In the passage before us, Paul assumes that the first object of agape is God (Romans 8:28), and the second object is our neighbor. Paul explains this *very* practically using terms and phrases such as, "be genuine," "hold fast," "show affection," "outdo one another" and "be aglow." A little further in this letter, Paul is even more emphatic when he says, "love [agape] one another; for he who loves his neighbor has fulfilled the law. [All] the commandments . . . are summed up in this sentence, 'You shall love your neighbor as yourself.' Love does no wrong to a neighbor; therefore love is the fulfilling of the law" (Romans 13:8-10).

Clearly this type of love (agape) demands the whole person. This love goes beyond family and friends to include the Church, the neighbor, the enemy, the world. We are to love because He loves us and made us children of the Father (Matthew 5:45). This is the agape that gives of the self without expecting a favor, reward or repayment. Why? Because Jesus said, "You . . . must be perfect, as your heavenly Father is perfect" (Matthew 5:48).

This perfection through love is void of popular "sloppy sentimentalism." Negatively, it cannot breed jealousy, egotism, irrational resentment. Rather, in a positive mode, it seeks the highest values of the human personality: truth, goodness, rightness, peacefulness and joy. In the presence of human imperfections, Christian love maintains belief in human nature, tolerance of injury and a true hope for human perfection. This is the love that surpasses all understanding — "the word of the cross [that] is folly to those who are perishing, but to us who are being saved it is the power of God" (1 Corinthians 1:18).

* * *

> *You know what hour it is, how it is full time now for you to wake from sleep. For salvation is nearer to us now than when we first believed; the night is far gone, the day is at hand. Let us then cast off the works of darkness and put on the armor of light . . . not in debauchery and licentiousness, not in quarreling and jealousy. But put on the Lord Jesus Christ, and make no provision for the flesh, to gratify its desires (Romans 13:11-14).*

These are the verses that gave us one of the great saints of Christendom, St. Augustine. Despairing, brooding and weeping over his life and the possibility of the

Christian faith, he heard a voice from next door saying, "Take up and read." He read these verses and immediately "the light of assurance poured into his heart," and he was launched on the road to becoming a new creation — and a great Christian thinker and defender.

These verses are powerful because they are an appeal to crisis. Paul is saying to the Christians in Rome, "The new age is here, so let this be your motivation for ethical seriousness." Throughout the history of Christianity, there has always been interest in the end time. This is partly due to the human frustration of living with life's mysteries *and* the biblical references to the end of the world (such as the Book of Revelation, Matthew 24-25, among others.)

The early Church accepted this atmosphere of crisis. The new age had begun and the present age was passing away. The two ages had clearly met (1 Corinthians 10:11). Paul even suggests to the Thessalonians that the end will come in only months (1 Thessalonians 4:13-5:11). Certainly the end would come within the life-span of living Christians (Matthew 24:34). But here Paul is less emphatic about the advent of Jesus, indicating a change of thinking. The day is almost here, but when it will arrive is known only by the Father (Matthew 24:36). So do not worry about the end, just stay awake and endeavor to live in the armor of light, in prayer, in agape and so in Jesus Christ. The equipment to do this is heavenly — the Spirit of Christ (Romans 9:9) who frees us from the flesh for newness of life (Romans 8:4-9).

Paul ends his Letter to the Roman Christians, whom he has yet to meet, with words of encouragement (Romans 15:1-13), some personal notes (15:14-23) and final greetings (chapter 16). Paul's list of individuals for greeting is lengthy, indicating the commonality of fellowship he shared with the Christians in Rome. This fellowship of Christians was vital to the body of Christ. This is practically suggested by Paul when he commends Phoebe, "a deaconess of the church at Cenchreae" (Romans 16:1), to the Roman Christians asking that they help her in any way necessary. It is well-known that ancient inns and lodging houses were often places where thieves and prostitutes gathered. As a result, early Christian travelers often depended upon fellow Christians for lodgings and accommodations. Such was the wonderful early fellowship network of the Mystical Body of Christ.

CHAPTER THREE

Paul's Letters
to the Corinthians

• Introduction

Corinth was a very strategic city in the history of the Greek nation. It was the connecting point between the Greek mainland and the Peloponnesus landmass to the south. Corinth also had two ports which offered access to two seas, the Aegean to the east and the Mediterranean to the west. In Paul's day it was an industrial, cultural, governmental and athletic center, with a cosmopolitan population from throughout the empire. Like every major port city, debauchery and licentiousness were very evident. It was clearly a "fast-paced" city.

Paul arrived in Corinth early in the year 51 (Acts 18:1). After initial difficulty (Acts 18:12-17) and with "fear and trembling" (1 Corinthians 2:3), he eventually ended some eighteen months of labor with a firmly established Church (2 Corinthians 1:1). Paul received assistance in Corinth from Priscilla and Aquila during what was for him a rather long ministry at this stage in his career (Romans 16:3-4; Acts 18:1-4). It appears that most of Paul's initial converts were uneducated poor folk (1 Corinthians 1:26-28), slaves (1 Corinthians 12:13 and 7:21) and common laborers, although a handful of educated individuals were members (1 Corinthians 1:14; Romans 16:23).

As with all of Paul's converts, during his absence he continued to help them and remained their spiritual guide and counselor. When he learned of spiritual strains, Paul wrote letters offering guidance and direction that substituted for his presence. Because of Corinth's "modernness" in every sense of the word, Paul's two letters are wonderful insights for current difficulties and problems of twentieth-century Christianity.

Historical Context

After leaving Corinth in late summer of 52, Paul visits Jerusalem a third time and then travels to Ephesus where he stays for three years. During his lengthy stay in Ephesus, Paul receives bad news from the Church at Corinth. As a result, he writes them a letter warning of immorality. This letter is noted by Paul in his First Epistle to the Corinthians, which states: "I wrote to you in my letter not to associate with immoral men. . . . I wrote to you not to associate with any one who bears the name of brother if he is guilty of immorality or greed, or is an idolater, reviler, drunkard, or robber — not even to eat with such a one" (5:9, 11). (Some scholars believe this epistle to be 2 Corinthians 6:14 and 7:1.)

"Chloe's people" (1 Corinthians 1:11), or Chloe's household, send reports (perhaps by letter, 1 Corinthians 7:1) that members of the Corinthian Church were squabbling among themselves, causing serious divisions (1 Corinthians 1:12-17). Even Paul's own apostolic authority was being questioned (1 Corinthians 1:11). Reports of these troubles also came to Paul from other sources, namely Stephanas, Fortunatus and Achaicus (1 Corinthians 16:17). Apparently these men came to Paul with an account of the troubles in Corinth seeking clarification and direction. The First Letter to the Corinthians appears to be Paul's response to the problems and developing tensions.

Not long after, Paul seems to have gotten word that his letter was not dealing with the situation. Perhaps the young Timothy, who came from Corinth to Ephesus (1 Corinthians 16:10), informed Paul of the continuing strains. The impulsive Paul apparently decides to pay a short visit to Corinth, although this visit is not recorded by Luke in Acts. Paul certainly implies such a visit when he writes, "For I made up my mind not to make you another painful visit" (2 Corinthians 2:1; also 2 Corinthians 12:14 where Paul writes, "Here for the third time I am ready to come to you"; see also 12:21 and 13:1). Without doubt this brief visit would have been a "painful" affair.

Upon returning to Ephesus, Paul sends a much stronger letter to the Corinthians by way of Titus. This second letter is written with "much affliction and anguish of heart and with many tears, not to cause you pain but to let you know the abundant love that I have for you" (2 Corinthians 2:4; some scholars believe this letter to be at least in part 2 Corinthians, chapters 10-13).

Paul then travels to Macedonia, having been forced to leave Ephesus because of a riot (Acts 20:1). In Macedonia Paul receives welcome news from Titus that tensions in Corinth have receded and their attitudes were much improved (2 Corinthians 7:5-13). He is told by Titus that the Corinthians long and mourn for a visit from Paul (2 Corinthians 7:7). The Corinthians had been "grieved into repenting" and "godly grief produces a repentance that leads to salvation" (2 Corinthians 7:9-11). Paul rejoices in all this, and sends back with Titus a substitute for his presence, the epistle we know as 2 Corinthians.

Paul's second New Testament Corinthian letter expresses his great joy over their spiritual well-being. (Many scholars believe this to be 2 Corinthians 1-9 or 2

Corinthians 1:1-6:13 and 7:2-9:15.) He is compassionate with regard to their past problems, but takes the opportunity to speak of other subjects that are important for the Christian community. He writes of preachers, parishioners, the Christian hope of life after death and his general understanding of salvation. If chapters 10-13 are of the same letter, Paul adds a section clarifying his apostolic authority. (Having noted various scholarly divisions of the Corinthian epistles, we will deal with the writings simply as presented by the New Testament canon, for the sake of clarity.)

Because the problems of the Corinthian Church are uncertain, we must briefly consider the gospel or the message Paul preached to the Corinthians. In this way we will be better positioned to understand the circumstances Paul seeks to address in his epistles. Paul had originally come to the Corinthians preaching fulfillment of the prophetic message through the death and resurrection of Jesus Christ. Through faith, baptism and the Eucharist believers could share in Christ's power over death and experience the world to come. This "day of salvation" (2 Corinthians 6:2) is made evident by God's Spirit being poured out on all people (Joel 2:28) — especially the body of Christ.

As a result, life in the early Church emphasized the Spirit of God. The kingdom of God which Jesus spoke of so often (Luke 4:43; 8:1; 9:11; 16:16; Matthew 8:17; 11:4-5; Mark 1:15; 1:27; and others) was synonymous with life in the Spirit. So Paul could speak of visions (2 Corinthians 12:1ff) and speaking the "tongues of angels" (1 Corinthians 13:1; see also Isaiah 28:11; this is ecstatic speech, or speaking in tongues). These were signs of the end. It is not surprising then to learn that Paul apparently spoke in tongues while in Corinth (1 Corinthians 14:18) and displayed other charismatic gifts. This appears to have caused some difficulty in the Corinthian Church because the end of time was slow in coming. As can happen with "gifts" of the Spirit, they became an end in themselves and so were thought to "cause" salvation rather than being the result of salvation. So Paul, receiving word of divisions, writes to reclaim the Corinthian Church.

Summary of Contents

Chloe's people (1 Corinthians 1:11) report to Paul the problems in their Church. There are claims to special religious knowledge, diverse leaders (Paul, Peter, Apollos and Christ!), and speaking in tongues as evidence of leadership. Little cliques developed in the congregation. Some even ate great quantities at the Eucharist thinking the end was near and as a result nothing was left for late arrivers — probably slaves (1 Corinthians 1:10-4:21). One member of the congregation was even living unashamedly with his stepmother (5:1-8, 13). Others attempted to settle disagreements among Christians by going to pagan officials (6:1-11).

Paul now addresses the matters concerning the Corinthians. In fact, Paul offers an outline of their letter if we assume he introduces each of their questions with the phrase, "Now concerning" (1 Corinthians 7:1, 25; 8:1; and 16:1). Paul then addresses marriage (chapter 7); living in the world (8:1-11:1); men and women in worship (11:2-16); spiritual gifts (chapters 12-14), and the resurrection (chapter 15).

In Paul's second epistle (following the New Testament), he responds to his "painful visit" (2 Corinthians 2:1). He offers (in what some consider his fourth letter) autobiographical data (1:12-2:17); a defense of his ministry (3:1-6:10); words of reconciliation (6:11-7:16), and his collection for the "poor" in Jerusalem (chapters 8-9). In chapter 10 (which some scholars consider to be his third letter, 10:1-13:13), Paul offers a defense of his authority and apostleship, concluding that he has every right to boast (10:12-18). Then Paul offers a justification for boasting (11:1; see also 12:13) and a plan for his pending visit (12:14; 13:10).

Passages for Everyday Living

Paul, called by the will of God to be an apostle of Christ Jesus . . . to the church of God which is at Corinth, to those sanctified in Christ Jesus, called to be saints together with all those who in every place call on the name of our Lord Jesus Christ, both their Lord and ours: Grace to you and peace from God our Father and the Lord Jesus Christ (1 Corinthians 1:1-3).

As Paul introduces himself to the readers at Corinth, he reveals his thoughts and interests for the epistles. He first emphasizes his call. He is called by the very will of God to speak and teach of Christ. To whom is he commissioned to speak? To the Church of God at Corinth. To those who are baptized into Christ, the Christ who puts us right with God. Sanctification is the making holy, through the life, death and resurrection of Christ, those who are called to be saints. Christianity is not without its ongoing, creative and developing "sanctity." All are called to form the "sacred congregation" because they call upon the name of the Lord (Psalm 99:6; Joel 2:32). Though the Corinthian Church may be divided, they were all one in Christ.

The words "sanctification" and "saint" are used in

the active sense throughout the Scriptures. Sanctification means making, or being made, holy. Hence, being chosen to be the people of God literally means being *made* the people of God. Paul is emphatic — there is no standing still in the Christian faith. Either we are moving forward or slipping backward. There is no point of rest. The spiritual person is either nourished or starved. Modern science, through the influence of Einstein, has taught that there is no point of absolute rest in the universe. There is only becoming; all is relative. The opposite of becoming is chaos. Paul is saying in effect, all of you who are traveling, progressing and maturing on your particular spiritual journey of faith, *you are* indeed the Church universal, the Church of God in Christ.

Paul is also clearly aware that we do not achieve this spiritual growth and maturity ourselves. Grace is a gift, free for the taking. Through the Holy Spirit, we grow into "Christlikeness." As Paul writes later, we ". . . beholding [or reflecting] the glory of the Lord, are being changed into his likeness from one degree of glory to another; for this comes from the Lord who is the Spirit" (2 Corinthians 3:18).

Then Paul gives his standard salutation (Romans 1:7), "Grace and peace." Grace indicates for Paul the *eternal* gift of God's favor and love in Christ. This grace is God's movement toward us *and* the establishing in believers a spiritual *charis* (grace) gift or spiritual talent (Romans 12:3-8). Peace is the Christian's well-being, assurance and quiet confidence he experiences because of his right relationship with God. Paul is quite clear that this "peace which passes all understanding" comes only from God (see Romans 1:7; 2 Corinthians 1:2; Galatians 1:3; Ephesians 1:2; Philippians 1:2; Colossians 1:2; and others). This is the peace that can never be taken from Christ's followers — not even those who face the ultimate temptation to abandon faith, that is, death. With this peace of God as his theme, John Keble once wrote these lines:

> Tis sweet, as year by year we lose
> Friends out of sight, in faith to muse
> How grows in Paradise our store.

Such is the peace of God that Paul knew so well, a peace that no Christian can be unaware or dismiss lightly.

* * *

> For Jews demand signs and Greeks seek wisdom, but we preach Christ crucified, a stumbling block to Jews and folly to Gentiles, but to those who are called, both Jews and Greeks, Christ the power of God and the wisdom of God (1 Corinthians 1:22-24).

Paul is careful to point out that the Gospel of Jesus Christ is not a new philosophy. This is not gnosticism, the Greek word *gnosis* meaning a special type of knowledge that gives assurance and salvation. No, the Gospel is a positive message of a God who loves His creation so much that He would go to extremes establishing fellowship with them. So the "cross is folly" to great minds of wisdom. Those who put their trust in this world's wisdom are perishing (verse 18). "Where is the wise man?" says Paul (verse 20). Where is the debater and the scribe? It is not wisdom that leads one to God! Rather it was God's free will to reveal himself in a manner which defies all worldly wisdom and philosophy. God was in Christ reconciling the world. In the eyes of the world, this is a foolish message! So here is not philosophy, but Good News to be believed and lived.

Paul indicates how all humanity has been in search for God. The Jews wanted some type of supernatural sign to ease their minds, and here Paul could speak from experience. This demand is not limited to the Jews; peoples of all ages and nations have demanded signs from God (or gods) from the beginning of time. "Are you there, God? Give me some indication!" is not an unusual request, especially when situations are desperate. The *Jerusalem* way would seem the normal way for one to seek and find God, the way of historical proof. But God chose another way.

The Greeks (or all humanity beyond the Jews) seek wisdom. They search for God with their minds seeking desperately to understand, to find the way of rationality. Humanity has often sought this way too, the way of *Athens*. For the Greeks, religion had to give account of itself philosophically by explaining the relationship between Creator and creature. But God chose another way.

Because the Gospel presents Christ crucified, the Jews and Greeks stumbled. They did not seek a "weak" sign, a "mysterious" death, as *the* way to God. Human instinct says to go another way. This is the crisis of faith; we either give up our search and rely totally upon God's work in Christ, or we abandon Christ and continue our search. Paul then refers to those who are *called*, or those who respond to the gift of grace by accepting Christianity. The called have given up their own search and followed the crucified One, who has become their Savior.

Ironically, those who give up their own individual search receive the very thing they are seeking. Although from the human side Christianity seems absurd, it fulfills the natural needs or searchings of humanity. Where we first sought a "sign," now comes the *power* of Christ; and where we initially sought human "wisdom," now comes the *wisdom* of God (1 Corinthians 1:24). Because this power and wisdom of God in Christ is so much greater than our potential creaturely achievements through human wisdom, our *peace* and assurance are unsurpassable.

This is the reason preaching or speaking the Good News seems like "sheer folly." In hearing the message, one has to follow or harden the heart to the promptings of the Holy Spirit. The Christian not only speaks the message of Jesus verbally, but also in the life one lives. As Paul so well knew, the faithful follower of Jesus must be prepared to face mockery, rejection, ridicule, and even aggression.

* * *

> *For I decided to know nothing among you except Jesus Christ and him crucified. . . . We impart this in words not taught by human wisdom but taught by the Spirit, interpreting spiritual truths to those who possess the Spirit. . . . "For who has known the mind of the Lord so as to instruct him?" But we have the mind of Christ (1 Corinthians 2:2-16).*

This entire second chapter of 1 Corinthians is deserving of careful reading and deep meditation. It speaks of profoundly spiritual things. The verses noted above somewhat outline the contents of the chapter and we shall use them in this manner.

At the beginning of the chapter, Paul gives all the credit to God. He did not come with "lofty words" and clever language. He deliberately decided that Christ was the only means of access and that he would come with no "outside" wisdom, that is, worldly wisdom. As St. John Chrysostom (archbishop of Constantinople, died 407) comments on this passage: "For I [Paul] came not weaving syllogisms nor sophisms, nor saying unto you anything else than Christ is crucified. . . . They indeed have ten thousand things to say . . . all of them I outstripped: which is a sign, such as no words can express, of the power of Him whom I preach."

Then Paul speaks of the work of the Spirit in this whole process. The Spirit of God inspires persons to speak of Him giving right message and right expression. These are not human morsels but heavenly portions. Paul's emphasis that the Spirit teaches these truths indicates some effort on behalf of the hearer. This refers to the initial hearer and the hearer who is taught by the one who initially hears. In each case, God has given a rationality for Christ's work and this cannot be ignored. Even though Paul is writing to brethren who were not "wise according to worldly standards" (1 Corinthians 1:26), the expectation of Christians is that they responsibly grow and mature in the power and wisdom of Christ.

Paul draws this all together with his profound statement, "but we have the mind of Christ." The truths surrounding the cross of Christ are the basic sound waves of the universe. As we turn time and again leaving behind our own sense of religious direction, trusting in the person Christ, we begin to thankfully reflect and live what He taught and lived. Quoting the Prophet Isaiah (40:13) that no one has directed or instructed God, Paul asserts that because Christ *is* God, we can now mirror the mind of Christ, that is, the will of God.

* * *

For we are God's fellow workers; you are God's field, God's building. . . . Do you not know that you are God's temple and that God's Spirit dwells in you? (1 Corinthians 3:9, 16).

Paul is interpreting the Gospel to the Corinthian Church in accord with their troubles. Having been concerned about divisions within the Church (3:3), Paul turns to their unity. All are one in Christ, as fellow workers, because God "gives the growth" (verse 7). Regardless of who plants or waters, only God is the common ground. Hence persons become "God's field" to be planted and "God's house" to be built. Paul does not want them to stay on milk or Pablum (3:2), but is keen that they grow and mature into the fullness of Christ. Christians belong to God, but all must grow in the faith. (See Jesus' teachings, for example: Luke 13:6-9; 14:34-35; Matthew 20:1-16; 24:45-51; Mark 4:26-29; and others.)

This growth is necessary because we are the temple of God (see also 1 Corinthians 5:19 for a very similar statement). If the Spirit of God dwells in us and we are in constant communion with the Father in Christ through the Spirit, it follows that a maturing process will occur. Relationships between persons reflect the same accent of growth. Unless they become more familiar and comfortable with each other, the relationship stagnates or dissolves. But Christians have the very Spirit of God saturating their being and making their bodies a "living sacrifice, holy and acceptable to God" (Romans 12:1). This is constant communion and fellowship.

Jesus emphasizes the same. The temple was a place of prayer (Mark 11:17). Further, Jesus suggested that prayer offered in spirit and truth transcended the temple (John 4:21-24). Hence Jesus spoke of replacing the temple with a spiritual posture, the body of the resurrected Christ (John 2:19-21; see also 1 Corinthians 12:27). This body of Christ, with its many member temples, is a place where God's Spirit dwells in deep communion and fellowship.

Do you not know that a little leaven leavens the whole lump? Cleanse out the old leaven that you may be a new lump, as you really are unleavened. For Christ, our paschal lamb, has been sacrificed. Let us, therefore, celebrate the festival, not with the old leaven, the leaven of malice and evil, but with the unleavened bread of sincerity and truth (1 Corinthians 5:6-8).

Paul uses leaven in the opposite way of the Gospels. In Jesus' teachings, it symbolizes the secretly growing kingdom of God (Matthew 13:44; Luke 13:20-21). For Paul, the leaven that influences the lump is the evil that can destroy the whole (Galatians 5:9). In Paul's sense, one must be unleavened or without the evil that Paul associates with the flesh (Romans 7). The difference is one of intention: Jesus *introduced* the kingdom of God whereas Paul is seeking to *preserve* the kingdom. Paul's apostolic ministry occurred at a time when the body of Christ was seeking to define its place in society, hence the negative use of leaven. In any case, the message remains the same.

Further, the Jewish custom was to destroy leaven (Exodus 12:15-16; 13:7). The paschal festival of the Jewish Passover was such a grand event, marking God's sparing of the Jewish people during their captivity in Egypt (Exodus 5:1; 11:4-9; 12:1-28). Drawing an important contrast between the sacrificial practices of the Jewish passover festival and the death of Christ, the "new" lamb of God, Paul writes that the Corinth Church celebrates not with the old leaven or covenant but with the new covenant of Christ. This new unleavened bread is of sincerity and truth, that is, trusting and clinging fully and completely to the death and resurrection of Christ. Through His work, evil is defeated.

It follows then that the Christian life should be a feast! It should be a full and joyous celebration of Christ's reconciling work. Now is begun a lasting peace between God and humanity which shall reach a final and magnificent glory (Philippians 4:4-7).

A greater, and the earlier, statement about the "feast" of the Lord's Supper, or the Eucharist, is found in 1 Corinthians 11:20-34. Here Paul warns against overeating and drunkenness during the Eucharist (verse 20) and then reiterates what he "received from the Lord" (verse 23). To misuse this meal is to profane "the body and blood of the Lord" (verse 27). Examine yourself prior to the meal (verse 28) — and if you are very hungry, "eat at home" (verse 34).

* * *

I mean, brethren, the appointed time has grown very short. . . . For the form of this world is passing away (1 Corinthians 7:29, 31).

Early in Paul's ministry, he seemed convinced that the end was near. The Lord may return at any moment. The followers of Jesus were to live as Jesus told them, watching and praying (Matthew 24:43-44; 25:1-13; Luke 12:41-48; Mark 13:24-27; and others). Because the values of this world are passing away, the Christian must remain detached from the world (see also 1 John 1:18; 2:15-17). Although the end has not yet come, this in itself indicates the seriousness of Paul's teachings. All Christians must take Jesus' teachings and Paul's warnings seriously. We must keep watch, pray and wait so the Master will find us *ready* (not just waiting!) when He comes. Hence Paul concludes this letter with the words,

"Our Lord, come!" (*marana-tha* in the Greek, 1 Corinthians 16:22).

* * *

> *Do you not know that in a race all the runners compete, but only one receives the prize? So run that you may obtain it. Every athlete exercises self-control in all things. They do it to receive a perishable wreath, but we an imperishable (1 Corinthians 9:24-25).*

What a lovely way to speak of the Christian life! In a fast-paced and culturally developed society — much like today — Paul speaks of self-denial and self-giving. Every two years Corinth held the Isthmian Games, similar to the present-day Olympics. A wreath of palm branches was given to the winners of these games, participants who were often of "professional" status. Paul's analogy would have registered with the Corinthian Church, as it should have meaning today: eternal life is a far greater reward than a trophy of withering branches! So train carefully, diligently, constantly and completely.

* * *

> *So, whether you eat or drink, or whatever you do, do all to the glory of God (1 Corinthians 10:31).*

Remember, writes Paul, you are no longer your own. You belong to Christ, do not seek to please yourself, but only the Father in heaven. Do not offend either Jew or Greek through eating habits, but do all for the building up of the body of Christ. In the previous verses, Paul says to follow his example, and following this verse he writes, "Be imitators of me, as I am of Christ" (11:1). The early Christian communities needed direction for living.

Paul's rule was simple: "Do all to the glory of God!"

* * *

> . . . *in the Lord woman is not indepen-*
> *dent of man nor man of woman; for as*
> *woman was made from man, so man is*
> *now born of woman. And all things are*
> *from God (1 Corinthians 11:11-12).*

Paul is thought to be the enemy of woman because of his suggestions that women be submissive to men (see Ephesians 5:22ff). Furthermore, women are not to be in authority (1 Timothy 2:12), they are to fulfill God's purpose, having children (1 Timothy 2:15); they are to be silent in church (1 Corinthians 14:34), and Paul himself chose to be celibate (1 Corinthians 7:7).

Many scholars now believe that much of this material comes from a later source than Paul himself. However, this eleventh chapter of Corinthians remains a problem. The verses before us are critical for understanding Paul's perception of women in the Christian faith (especially for understanding 1 Corinthians 11:7). Paul writes here of human *origins* established by God at creation. This is the order that the Church should respect. The emphasis is on both male *and* female as responsible before God in their distinctive roles. Dominance is not the primary issue, but the natural response of God from one's "sexual" station in life. Paul then was neither a chauvinist nor a women's liberationist, but one seeking to encourage stability in the early Church. As a result, women's role in the Church remains an issue to be clarified.

* * *

> *Now concerning spiritual gifts,*
> *brethren, I do not want you to be unin-*

formed. . . . Therefore I want you to understand that no one speaking by the Spirit of God ever says "Jesus be cursed!" and no one can say "Jesus is Lord" except by the Holy Spirit (1 Corinthians 12:1, 3).

Paul now launches into a lengthy discussion of spiritual gifts. This was obviously an important issue in the early Corinthian Church and has become an issue at various times throughout the history of Christianity. In chapters 12, 13 and 14 of 1 Corinthians, Paul instructs the Corinthian Church thusly: first, on the receiving of gifts, which can be tested by determining whether they are for the good of the whole community (12:1-11); second, on the body of Christ, which has many members, each bringing a gift or gifts to the community (12:12-31); third, on the greatest gift of all, which is love (13); and fourth, on the usefulness of speaking in tongues (14:1-40).

Corinth apparently had a group in the Church who emphasized a very emotional and ecstatic type of worship experience. Paul seems to be concerned that an internal division will occur through one group's "enthusiasm" and earnest spiritual goals. Thrilling rapture must not divide the body of Christ. What criteria can be used to distinguish Christ's Spirit from the human spirit? Paul writes that the person who says — and lives the phrase — "Jesus is Lord," attests to the indwelling of the Holy Spirit. Traditionally this has always been a difficulty for the Church. But eventually life-style, sincerity and general truthfulness witness to the Spirit's presence and one's living to the glory of God (rather than self).

Then Paul speaks of the variety of gifts and services stemming from the same Spirit and Lord. He makes a point to state that *all* have these gifts (verse 7), a clear result of believing in Christ and being "possessed" by the

Spirit. But whether the gift be one of utterance, faith, a type of healing, the working of miracles (literally "active powers" in the Greek), prophecy, discernment, the speaking of a foreign tongue or an interpreter of a foreign tongue (verses 8-11), Paul carefully emphasizes that the gift is manifested for *the common good of all*. The gift is not for self-display, self-enjoyment or individual use. It is solely for enhancing one's relationship to God *and* serving the body of Christ.

Paul emphasizes this usage by referring to the body of Christ and its many members. Unity is again the theme. If a foot, ear, and so on, refuse to be a part of the body because they are not another part, the body would be incomplete and handicapped. Likewise, if every person was an eye, there would be no body of Christ (1 Corinthians 12:14-26).

What a superb analogy for asserting the *importance of every member*. All are called, and of those responding to a new and exciting relationship with God, they are molded into the mystery of Christ through the common Spirit — all believers become adopted children of the Father, members of the one body. "God arranged the organs in the body, each one of them, as he chose" (12:18). We are where we are by divine appointment! This is not to say the assignment cannot be changed, that new orders cannot be given. This comes through prayer and worship. Hence Augustine could write, "He cannot have God for his father who refuses to have the church for his mother!"

Adding a section suggesting posts for service in the Church (1 Corinthians 12:27-30), Paul turns to "a still more excellent way" (verse 31). In the midst of discussing spiritual gifts, Paul says the greatest gift of all is *love* (chapter 13). Here is one of the most profound chapters in the Scriptures. Not the "thing" but the gift all

Christians have is love (*agapē* in the Greek). This love is supernatural, a gift of the Spirit of God. It reflects God's love for us in Christ and can never be replaced or made secondary. Without love, no gift — however great it may seem — is of any value or importance. The logical conclusion? Without agape, no one can claim to be a Christian. "So faith, hope, love abide, these three; but the greatest of these is love" (1 Corinthians 13:13).

Then Paul turns his attention to speaking in tongues (chapter 14). Paul's argument is that because prophecy edifies the body of Christ, it is perferred to glossolalia, or speaking in tongues (verses 4-5). It is clear that the Corinth Church relied heavily upon speech for its worship (1:5; 12:8, 28).

Inspired speech, prayer and song played a significant role in their gatherings. But glossolalia was inarticulate (not inaudible) and often resulted in a state of unconsciousness for the one speaking. These utterances need to be interpreted or they are of no value. Paul concludes that if there is no one to interpret the glossolalia during worship, "let each of them keep silence in church and speak to himself and to God" (14:28). As John Chrysostom writes on these verses, to practice glossolalia under any other criteria is to deprive God His glory and "bring shame upon those who have them [unconscious states] in the eyes of the unbelievers."

* * *

. . . Christ died for our sins in accordance with the scriptures, that he was buried, that he was raised on the third day in accordance with the scriptures, and that he appeared to Cephas, then to the twelve. Then he appeared to more than five hundred brethren at one time, most of

whom are still alive, though some have
fallen asleep (1 Corinthians 15:3-6).

Here is the substance and heart of Paul's Gospel. Not
only is this the earliest written reference to the resurrection of Christ (this letter was written before the
Gospels), but here is the essential ingredient of the
Christian belief. If Christ is not risen, there is no Christian message! Apparently some members of the Corinthian Church did not believe in the resurrection of the
body, an idea inherent within Greek philosophy (especially Plato). Where does one look to deal with this issue?
Paul goes right to the source — the risen and living
Christ whom he met so vividly on the Damascus road.
This is the place of truth witnessed by those chosen of
God.

If Christ is not risen, asserts Paul, those who live by
faith and we who preach that Christ lives are fools. In
fact, God is being misrepresented. Paul's logic is unrelenting: ". . . we testified of God that he raised Christ,
whom he did not raise if it is true that the dead are not
raised. For if the dead are not raised, then Christ has not
been raised" (1 Corinthians 15:15-16). Either Christ is
raised or life is futile and without a future.

But He lives! This is the Easter message and Paul's
emphasis in verses 20-28. Christ's resurrection is a fact
within time and space. It is a historical reality. With this
status, it can do nothing less than change the course of
history, from rebellious and declining history to "salvation history." All who are baptized in Him reap the reward of eternal life.

Paul's method is vital. When dealing with the difficult area of life after death and future existence, Paul
does not turn to any other source but Christ. When death
approaches, when the end of life draws near for self or

another, Paul says, "Look to the living and resurrected Christ." As a Christian, do not look first to the dead or dying body, nor to the loss, nor to the tomb, nor to the emptiness of death; look first and always to the resurrected Christ. He has overcome the death of the body. He has won a stunning and irreversible victory. Oh, what joy and peace to be released from death! "It is sown a physical body, it is raised a spiritual body" (1 Corinthians 15:44).

Then Paul deals with the sticky issue of how we will be raised. Christians will be raised like Christ, in some type of spiritual-physical body. The completeness of our being will be fully realized only in Christ. "For now we see in a mirror dimly, but then face to face" (1 Corinthians 13:12). As with Christ's body, our bodies will be changed and transformed in accordance with the conditions of the "new" life.

Following Paul's method, we find clues to this new life when we consider the resurrected Christ. He passed through doors (Luke 24:36-38; John 20:19-20); encouraged the disciples to touch His "new" flesh and bones (Luke 24:39); He encouraged Thomas to touch His wounds (John 20:26-29); He ate fish and possibly bread (Luke 24:41-43 and perhaps Luke 24:30-31), and He mysteriously parted from the disciples (or ascended to heaven, Luke 24:51; Acts 1:9). In contrast, He told Mary not to touch Him (John 20:17) and He was not immediately recognizable (John 20:15-16; 21:4-14; Luke 24:13-35).

What an exciting and inspiring glimpse of life after death we find in these passages. In Christ the door to eternity opens just a wee crack and we see a life of spiritual-physical wholeness and totality. It is no wonder that the resurrection of Jesus was on all the lips of early Christians — especially at the Eucharist. The current troubles and difficulties of this life could not be compared to the life that was to come. This is the excitement Paul communicates in this chapter of Corinthians, and this is why to this day it remains a primary text for burials and funerals. Hence Paul could write later to the Corinthian Church: "We all, . . . beholding the glory of the Lord, are being changed into his likeness from one degree of glory to another; for this comes from the Lord who is the Spirit" (2 Corinthians 3:18). Eventually we shall be like Him, resurrected and in glory.

* * *

Blessed be the God and Father of our Lord Jesus Christ, the Father of mercies and God of all comfort, who comforts us in all our affliction, so that we may be able to comfort those who are in any affliction, with the comfort with which we ourselves are comforted by God. For as we share abundantly in Christ's sufferings, so through Christ we share abundantly in comfort too (2 Corinthians 1:3-5).

The word "comfort" is a favorite of Paul in this epistle. He uses the word seven times (and only thirteen in all his letters) and it carries the meaning of "divine refreshment." The Greek words used by Paul in the passage above indicate that God's refreshment of us is to be shared with others who need God's comfort.

Jesus uses the Greek word "comfort" when He says, "Blessed are those who mourn, for they shall be *comforted*" (Matthew 5:4; emphasis added). The meaning is consolation; the wiping away of tears for those who are distressed or having difficulties. This comfort comes through Christ (who has suffered) and the Holy Spirit, the *Great Comforter* (John 14:16-17, 25-27; 15:26;

16:13-14; the Greek word has been translated "Holy Spirit," the literal transliteration as paraclete, possibly as Spirit of Truth and comforter). The word has great significance for Paul.

The terms consolation and comfort are found throughout Paul's letters. They tell of God's love and care for those who journey through life. There will be suffering and affliction on the journey home. God is not only *aware* of the hardships and difficulties we face, but the implication is that He *goes with us* — He does not leave us alone in the far country to make it home as best we can. But Paul, following Jesus, makes it clear that we are to help others during our travels (Matthew 18:21-35). Never are we solo travelers. The opportunity will always be there to share the comfort we receive from the Father. ". . . As you did it to one of the least of these my brethren, you did it to me" (Matthew 25:40).

* * *

For all the promises of God find their Yes in him. That is why we utter the Amen through him, to the glory of God (2 Corinthians 1:20).

God's promises in the Old Testament are fulfilled in Christ. This had great significance for Paul and the early Church because it meant God is faithful. His promises are true and will not go wanting. When God promises to come again; when He promises we shall be with Him in paradise; when He promises to prepare a room for us, we can be sure His promises will be completed. Promises translate as *yes* in Christ and now the Church can say, "amen" (see 1 Corinthians 14:16 for the early Church practice). In the Book of Revelation, Christ is called the "amen," "the beginning of God's creation"

(Revelation 3:14; see also 7:12). Hence when we say "amen," we are literally saying, "Christ — the key to everything."

* * *

But thanks be to God, who in Christ always leads us in triumph, and through us spreads the fragrance of the knowledge of him everywhere. For we are the aroma of Christ to God among those who are being saved and among those who are perishing (2 Corinthians 2:14-15).

Here is Paul's "Jewish" way of saying how God is glorified. The burning of the sacrifice in the Old Testament was thought to be sweet-smelling to God, a sacrifice given for His glory (Genesis 8:20-21; Exodus 29:18; Ezekiel 20:41; Malachi 3:4). Paul's work in Christ is something given for "God's glory." It is also worth noting that when a Roman general returned to Rome triumphant, many on the parade route would burn incense to "his glory."

All Christians are called to ministry in some respect. This is why they are given a gift or gifts of the Spirit. This is the Christian's equipment for the journey of faith, the journey that "in Christ always leads us in triumph" (2 Corinthians 2:14). Through the sweet fragrance of a Christian's work to the glory of God, others come to hear the Good News of Christ. We, as the body of Christ, are His hands, feet, tongue and eyes. Christians are the "aroma of Christ to God," living a life of sacrifice and giving. The result is a double-edged sword, because the Gospel of God's grace makes people choose to either be in correct relationship with God and follow Him (life), or have no relationship with God (death).

* * *

. . . We walk by faith, not by sight. . . .
For the love of Christ controls us, because
we are convinced that one has died for all;
therefore all have died. . . . if any one is in
Christ, he is a new creation; . . . we are
ambassadors for Christ. . . (2 Corinthians
5:7-20).

Throughout this section Paul is attempting to give a
defense of his ministry. In doing this he offers a rather
full picture of the motives and sufferings of a true follower of Christ.

Paul senses clearly his weakness in the flesh. But he
is driven by his new creaturehood established in the resurrected Christ for pointing toward the Christ. He emphasizes that we must walk — not stand still or just believe *but walk* — in faith. Faith is a gift from God. The
receiving of the gift means the use of the gift. Sight demands less commitment, faith demands the whole self.
"So be full of courage," says Paul, "because even though
we would rather be with the Lord, we have a job to do.
We are his body and must work accordingly" (see 2 Corinthians 5:6-10).

The motive of the Christian is twofold — love and
ambassadorship. Although Christians have to accept
their "distance" or temporary absence from the Lord,
we are literally controlled by the love of Christ. Because
He first loved us (and Paul!), we either love Him back
(like Paul!) or reject Him. There is no lukewarmness.
This agape (love) controls our whole being, life and values. As a result, we are motivated to act as His ambassador. Christians are God's instruments. As Paul, every believer is given the grace to tolerate all the limita-

tions of the flesh in order to be His representative — a natural response to He who *first* loved us.

It follows then that Christians are new creations. They are radically changed and become a clear influence in their particular station in life. The effects are in proportion to the calling (Romans 6:4; Galatians 6:15; Ephesians 4:24; Colossians 3:19). The newness is not limited to life-style, morality or ideology, but literally means the whole person. For Paul, being united to Christ means an all-new you! ". . . the old has passed away . . . the new has come" (2 Corinthians 5:17).

* * *

For godly grief produces a repentance that leads to salvation and brings no regret, but worldly grief produces death (2 Corinthians 7:10).

Paul wonderfully summarizes the basic teachings of the Gospel. Until one realizes his or her inability to put right the broken relationship between God and humanity; until one accepts his or her bankruptcy before God, having nothing to offer Him but filthy rags, salvation is unrealized. But once the need for this type of repentance is realized and acted upon, it leads to salvation. There will be no regret, as the "new" life is so brilliant and complete that it outshines any possible alternative. Paul does not speak of the psychological state of remorse, of being "spiritually" depressed and sorry for one's sins. He does not speak of wallowing in self-pity and emptiness. Repentance is necessary for salvation, but then the exciting and dynamic relationship with God allows no possibility for remorse. There is too much to be done for entertaining regrets. Rather, sorrow leads to a change of situation, from death to life. Paul speaks here of life that follows (daily?) repentance, just as day follows night.

For you know the grace of our Lord Jesus Christ, that though he was rich, yet for your sake he became poor, so that by his poverty you might become rich (2 Corinthians 8:9).

Grace, or *charis*, is the love of God for humanity. Paul states clearly that it is Jesus Christ who was equal with God or the same as God, that is, eternally "rich." He gave himself, He gave up all He had in order to make us eternally rich. The contrasting thoughts of richness and poverty are possibly triggered by Paul's discussion of an offering for the Jerusalem Church (Galatians 2:1-10; 1 Corinthians 16:1-4; Romans 15:25-27). After discussing this for several verses (2 Corinthians 8:1-7), he suddenly inserts a profound theological statement.

For Paul, the relationship between the mundane (the offering) and the spiritual (Christ's saving work) is inseparable. There cannot be one without the other. Like the liturgy, prayer, faith, work, human friendships, family relationships, the mundane or daily part of everyday living cannot be separated from the spiritual. For Paul, the ordinary, the uninteresting, the usual, are the arenas of God's natural expression of character and power. In the midst of daily things, Paul compresses the most profound thought and assertion of Scripture: that God became incarnate (took poverty), and made atonement (made humanity potentially rich), by reconciling all humanity to the Father. Here is stated Paul's important conviction that Jesus was God and not merely a specially blessed or gifted person. So is God's grace.

* * *

Examine yourselves, to see whether you are holding to your faith. Test your-

selves. Do you not realize that Jesus Christ is in you? (2 Corinthians 13:5).

Paul is exclaiming that those in Christ have God's approval. All are justified in God's sight when we are viewed through Christ. However, no person can be absolutely certain that God will *finally* approve them and their lives (1 Corinthians 3:10-15; Romans 14:10; 2 Corinthians 5:10; also see 1 Corinthians 9:27). Hence the Corinthians should "examine" themselves to be sure Christ is living within them. "Christ in you" is not a reference to a literal physical presence, but Christ through the Holy Spirit communicates to Christians the divine life. As St. Athanasius wrote in the fourth century, "But by virtue of the union of the Word with it [humanity], it [humanity] was no longer subject to corruption according to its own nature, but by reason of the Word that was come to dwell in it it was placed out of the reach of corruption."

The Christian "proves" the will of God. Because serious followers of the Christ live a "real" relationship with the living God, they are the new creation filled with the Spirit of God (1 Corinthians 2:6-16; Romans 12:2; Philippians 1:10). The spiritual insight of the Christian is a gift from God through Christ and in the Spirit. Hence a living dialogical relationship with God not only allows Christians to know the will of God but also to "work out . . . [their] own salvation with fear and trembling" (Philippians 2:12), that is, determine to an extent their own spiritual situation and condition.

Paul's use of "prove" and "testing" are important terms. To prove does not mean a rational argument, appealing to one's religious experience or some other absolute test of faith. Paul is instructing the Corinthians on the theme of behavior. In effect, he is saying, "Prove your Christian status by asking whether your behavior is fully consistent with your new and living relationship with God." If you really are in right relationship with God, then your behavior should reflect this communion. In fact, your behavior is a good *test* which indicates how well you are maintaining your relationship with God.

It is important to notice that for Paul, right conduct is not a means of establishing a right relationship with God. What is essential to the Christian faith is not good conduct but a *living fellowship*. Paul argues that regardless of how decent, noble and good our behavior and conduct, it does not count toward a right relationship with God (see Romans 4:1-8 and 5:1-11 where Paul is emphatic about justification through faith in Christ alone). But as a consequence of that right communion established through Christ and the Spirit, Paul says some alteration in conduct should occur as you maintain *this relationship* from your side of things. Paul concludes his letter with the words: "The grace of the Lord Jesus Christ and love of God and the fellowship of the Holy Spirit be with you all" (2 Corinthians 13:14).

Paul's Letter to the Galatians

As noted in a previous chapter, Paul's Letter to the Galatians is possibly his first epistle. If the term "Galatians" refers to the converts in the south of Asia Minor (present-day southeastern Turkey), Paul and Barnabas evangelized there during their first missionary journey (Acts 13:14, 51 and 14:6) and visited again on their second missionary journey (Acts 16:1-2). Written then about the year 47 or 48 (the alternate date of writing would be in the early 50s), it would have been sent from Paul's base at Antioch in Syria, and is directed at the controversy, namely, of how the Jewish and Christian faiths are related.

Historical Context

Saul and Barnabas are directed by the Holy Spirit to be "set apart." Probably through a prophetic utterance while fasting, the Church at Antioch receives the message that Saul and Barnabas are to do "the work to which I have called them" (Acts 13:2). Paul may have already sensed the possibilities of proclaiming the Gospel message to the territories surrounding Antioch because he had already preached in Cilicia, north of Antioch, prior to his association with Barnabas and the Antioch mission.

Paul then sets off on his first missionary journey along with Barnabas, the native Cyprian. They take with them John Mark, Barnabas's young cousin, whose mother was Mary. It was at Mary's home that the first Jerusalem Church met: the group which Peter led in the early days after the crucifixion-resurrection events (Acts 12:12). John Mark would have been a good choice for such a missionary project.

Luke tells us that "after fasting and praying they laid their hands on them and sent them off" (Acts 13:3). The threesome set off for Cyprus and then on to Pisidia. Their experiences are recorded in Acts 13-14. In the various cities they visited, their general plan was to go on the first Sabbath to the Jewish synagogue and if possible address the community with a word of exhortation or a homily (Acts 13:14-16). The "God-conscious" of the local synagogue congregations seem to have been attracted to Paul's message (for an example of his speaking, see Acts 13:16-41) and passed it on to their Gentile friends. Hence, for example, the week after Paul's preaching in Antioch of Pisidia, more Gentiles than Jews arrived at the synagogue to hear Paul speak (Acts 13:42-45). As a result, the Gentiles listened to Paul and Barnabas and "were glad and [they] glorified the word of God; and as many as were ordained to eternal life believed" (Acts 13:48). Then Luke tells us that "the word of the Lord spread throughout the region," even touching those "of high standing" so that when Paul and Barnabas left the city, "the disciples [in Antioch] were filled with joy and with the Holy Spirit" (Acts 13:49-52).

The Gentile converts, especially in Pisidian Antioch (Acts 13) and Iconium (Acts 14), created monumental problems for the early Christians. This first real crisis of the early followers of Jesus seems to have been unexpected. Apparently Gentile converts had been added to various synagogues so that they became familiar with the hope of Israel. When Paul and Barnabas came along and spoke their message, the Gentiles probably had less a sense of the tradition of the Jewish people than a born Jew would have felt. As a result, the "new" message was attractive and they told their Gentile friends to come and hear Paul, those friends not connected with the Jewish synagogue. However, the staunch Jewish leaders of the local synagogue were telling the Gentiles that they had to become proselytes to Judaism before they could worship the true God of the messiah Jesus.

Paul from the beginning assured these Gentile "converts" of the grace of God (evident in his message). The hope of Israel was fulfilled in the person Jesus and through faith in Him they too could receive the grace of God the same as their Jewish neighbors. In the new fellowship of people who believed in Jesus, there is no difference between a Jewish or Gentile person. So, would these friends of Gentile Jews be required to join the synagogue in order to become Christians? The crisis was developing in these early years, about 47 and 48.

Around the time of the council in Jerusalem (48 or 49), Paul learns of the "Gentile controversy." The apostolic council meeting in Jerusalem was to sort out this very problem (see Acts 15). Unable to visit the Church fellowships established on his recent missionary journey, Paul writes an urgent and strong epistle from his home base of Antioch. In the letter he addresses the situation quite clearly.

In the very first chapter (Galatians 1:7), Paul refers to "some agitators" who had questioned Paul's authority as an Apostle. Probably they accused him of not receiving his commission direct from Christ and therefore argued he could not be speaking the true message of

Jesus. Paul was not respecting Jewish tradition (the Mosaic law and circumcision) and was therefore diluting the Gospel. The confusion must have been great. Who is in charge — Paul or these teachers of a "different gospel"?

Paul writes defending his authority as an Apostle and in the process offers us some important personal data. He then emphasizes the new freedom found in the Gospel message asserting that his is the only true Gospel — that we have freedom only in Christ. Paul's message of Christian freedom is so emphatic throughout that Martin Luther referred to the letter to the Galatians as "the great epistle of freedom." Paul makes it quite clear that there are no strings attached to belief in Jesus Christ.

The opponents of Paul have come to be known as the Judaizers. They apparently were Christians, but they combined their faith with a strict Jewish background that even set them apart from "Jewish Christians." Perhaps they were of Pharisaic background (see Acts 15:5, for example), interested in only a portion of the law (Galatians 5:2-3) or perhaps they were religiously related to the mystics of nearby Colossae who worshiped "elemental spirits of the universe" (Galatians 4:3, 9; Colossians 2:8, 20) and observed sacred pagan festivals (Galatians 4:10). Regardless, Paul sensed the danger and wrote to put right the situation asserting that his Gospel was not second-hand, watered-down or ineffective.

Paul struggles in this letter with what one could perhaps call the first distortion or heresy of the Christian faith. If the centrality of the *person* Jesus Christ could be compromised by the addition of several "other" requirements, then the grace of God in Christ is lost. Only when one relies upon this grace alone is one a true member of the body of Christ. Paul had to respond.

Summary of Contents

After the normal address and salutation (Galatians 1:1-5), Paul takes no time for "thank yous." He goes right to the heart of the matter. He expresses astonishment at their desertion (1:6-9) and after cursing his rivals (1:7-9) he begins defending his apostleship (1:10 and 2:21). Paul held together as the two sides of one coin his apostolic commission and the truth of his Gospel. Paul argues his Gospel is not from any human person nor from the leaders of the Jerusalem Church. Indeed, on one occasion he even rebuked Peter because of their disagreement over the Gospel (2:11).

Then Paul launches into a full-blown defense of his Gospel (chapters 3 and 4). Appealing to Scripture (the Old Covenant, or Testament), Paul turns to Abraham asserting that through him God promised to bless all nations (that is, Gentiles). The greatness of Abraham rests not on his practice of circumcision (Genesis 17:9-11), but in his *faith* which "he reckoned it to him as righteousness" (Genesis 15:6). Faith preceded circumcision. Now, it is through faith in Christ, the one and true offspring of Abraham (Galatians 3:16), that the Gentiles become true sons of Abraham. Not even the law, which came hundreds of years after the covenant with Abraham, can help (3:17-18). For Paul, to not fully trust the Gospel was to not fully trust the God who gave it to humanity. Changes, additions or alterations are not possible.

Finally, Paul applies the Gospel (chapters 5 and 6). Christians must be responsible in the use of their freedom. They must stand fast (5:1-12), love their neighbor (5:13-25) and live the new law — the law of Christ (5:26-6:10).

Paul concludes with some personal comments (6:11-18) to his children in the faith.

Passages for Everyday Living

> *Paul an apostle — not from men nor through man, but through Jesus Christ and God the Father, who raised him from the dead — and all the brethren who are with me, to the churches of Galatia: Grace to you and peace from God the Father and our Lord Jesus Christ, who gave himself for our sins to deliver us from the present evil age, according to the will of our God and Father; to whom be the glory for ever and ever. Amen (Galatians 1:1-5).*

The opening sentences of Paul's letter gives us an indication of his thoughts as he begins to write. This is especially true in Galatians. Paul's immediate use of the term "apostle" is a clear indication of his thinking. He senses a need to clarify his commission and authority as an ambassador for Jesus Christ. He will not allow his enemies to question his calling, and from the outset seeks to put the record straight.

The Greek word *apostolos* is somewhat rare prior to New Testament usage. It literally means to "be sent forth." Jesus, in referring to His ministry, quotes the Old Testament Prophet Isaiah, "He has sent me" (Luke 4:16-18). Jesus repeats this commission often (Mark 9:37; Matthew 15:24; and others) and sends forth His followers as *Apostles*, those who "are sent forth." Although the word "Apostle" at first probably only applied to the original twelve followers of Jesus, it was eventually used to designate all who are called — like Paul — and "sent forth."

In light of Paul's stated apostleship, we can notice two points he makes.

First, one is called by the resurrected and living Jesus Christ. Paul's starting point is clear. He is an Apostle *because* he is called by Jesus Christ. Paul met Jesus on the Damascus road — he really met the One whom the Father raised from the dead. According to Paul, this is the heart of the Christian faith, this is the essence of the kingdom of God, this is the foundation of the Church. The center of it all is a *person*, one who lives.

Second, it is because of Jesus Christ that Paul can offer "grace and peace" to the many Churches of Galatia. This person, this God, in whose image we are made, is the only true source of peace and grace. By *grace* Paul means "God's favor," and acceptance of us who have turned away from our original purpose, or fellowship with God. Grace allows things to be right again. By *peace*, Paul means something like spiritual security. "Is it peace?" was a Hebrew greeting (see Judges 18:15, for example). Jesus was literally called the Prince of Peace, the Messiah, who put things right between humanity and God — and so, delivering "us from the present evil age" (Galatians 1:4). Both grace and peace are the result of a right and living relationship with the risen and active person Jesus Christ.

Here is the reason for Paul's letter. Here too is the Good News, the Gospel message of Christianity. At the beginning of the epistle, Paul's thoughts are clearly focused on the truth of the matter, that the joy of grace and peace are for all who accept a right relationship with God through Jesus Christ.

* * *

But when he who had set me apart
before I was born, and had called me
through his grace, was pleased to reveal
his Son to me, in order that I might preach

116

him among the Gentiles, I did not confer
with flesh and blood. . . (Galatians 1:15-16).

Here is the secret history of Paul's conversion, his experience of the inner revelation. In Paul's meeting of Jesus Christ on the Damascus road, his inner perception and understanding are jolted so severely that his life is changed and he was never the same. What a comfort, what reassurance are Paul's words of personal testimony. God not only draws individuals into a personal relationship, but He does not leave them alone. He does not leave them without further experience of His grace and peace. A living relationship between two individuals is always held in check by constant and continual experience. Although we may ignore the other person or take him or her for granted occasionally, a new experience renews the relationship. Paul's life indicates the same with regard to our relationship with God. He does not leave us alone — His costly love will not abandon us.

Paul's inner revelatory experience indicates three things.

First of all, our *destiny* is in God's hands. Paul refers to him "who had set me apart before I was born." This reminds us of the Psalmist's words: "For thou didst form my inward parts, thou didst knit me together in my mother's womb. . . . Thou knowest me right well; . . . Thy eyes beheld my unformed substance; in thy book were written, every one of them, the days that were formed for me, when as yet there was none of them" (Psalms 139:13-18). God's attention for us is not based on His moods but is eternal — before and after our life lived. God's presence and compassion are promised and God's hand can be traced in lives, especially in Paul's! For this Apostle, God is the creator and sustainer of life during our brief sojourn in this His world. Hence our destiny is

117

not left to chance. We are given a span of time to live, places to go and persons to know. How our destiny evolves will depend upon how prayerfully and carefully we seek to discover and follow the will of God for ourselves. As with Paul, so with us. Our lifelong task is to seek out His will in a living relationship with the resurrected Jesus Christ.

Second, it follows that we all have a *calling*. Like Paul, we are "called through his grace" to a particular vocation inclusive of people we meet, everyday tasks to be done and practical work to be fulfilled. Only we can influence and deal with the peculiar complex combination of *our* life's circumstances. We need to pray often to God: "Thank You that I can *uniquely worship* You today amidst my particular circumstances." Too seldom we feel God has forgotten us and we have no work to accomplish, no assignment to do. We sense we are "on the shelf!" But as Paul indicates, our destiny before God betrays a calling, and our calling must be worked out in our living relationship with God each day, each moment.

Third, we all have a *mission* in life. If we accept God's full awareness and compassion of our existence or destiny expressed so clearly by Paul and the Psalmist, then our practical vocation has a deeper purpose, and that is to "go tell it on the mountain" that Jesus Christ is Lord. Each individual does this daily in the life he lives, the things he says, in the thoughts he thinks. A well-known simple rhyme states this rather profoundly:

> *I am my neighbor's Bible, he reads me*
> *   when we meet;*
> *Today he reads me in my home, tomorrow*
> *   in the street.*
> *He may be relative or friend, or slight*
> *   acquaintance be;*

*He may not even know my name, yet he is
reading me.*

All of this stems, as Paul indicates, from a living fellowship with God that precedes and follows our "hand full" of days on earth. In all his writing, Paul is quite clear of his starting point. It is not himself, his own experience, his own thoughts, his own circumstances. The origination and source of his Christian faith is God in Jesus Christ. True to the Old Testament, it is always God who acts first so that humanity may respond. In thinking about our destiny, our calling and our mission, we must, like Paul, always begin with God, subjecting our feelings, moods and thoughts to the One who "sends forth," the One who sent forth His own Son.

* * *

*I have been crucified with Christ; it is
no longer I who live, but Christ who lives
in me; and the life I now live in the flesh I
live by faith in the Son of God, who loved
me and gave himself for me (Galatians
2:20).*

Here is stated the power of God in our lives. It is a real, living and energetic power because of Christ's historical crucifixion and death. His death is a fact. Now, because He died, Paul's inner spiritual self is transformed and remade. A total rebuilding occurs so that the old self is crucified. Old desires, old rebellious ways, old psychological mind-sets are torn down or crucified so the old "I" is replaced by the new values and concerns of Christ. Christ's primary concern was to do the will of the Father and this for Paul becomes the import, or purpose, of his new life.

What turned Paul into a new inner creature was not severe psychological depression or some great personal loss. Paul was touched by the love of God expressed for humanity — and thus for himself — in the historical death of Jesus Christ. Although some individuals are more open to the love of God in Christ when they experience some tremendous loss, anxiety or depression, for Paul it is clearly the *sacrificing love* of God that remade his inner person. When life goes well, people are distracted from the wonder of God's love. But in the end, it is always the power of God in Christ through the Holy Spirit that draws us to fellowship with Him; a living give-and-take relationship that redirects our very self. This is the fact and truth of God's love that is not limited by our psychological attitudes or blindness. Hence Paul is not despairing but rejoicing when he says "it is no longer I who live."

Paul now lives by *faith*. The roots of the Greek word for faith are found in the Hebrew prophets and psalmists — the essence of Paul's educational training as a Pharisee. In the Old Testament, faith is used in the passive sense of "faithfulness." For Paul, Jesus Christ is the incarnate faithfulness of God (see Romans 3:22, 25, for example). Faith is faith in God's faithfulness. God is the object of faith because He is faithful and loving to His creation. Paul lives "by faith in the Son of God" who died that the Apostle may be remade inside.

For early Christians then, faith can be understood as belief, trust, faithfulness and loyalty. Faith is active and passive, as evident in any relationship from friendship to marriage. It is the access to a living fellowship when one has faith in another and is faithful to the other. This is the channel of blessing, peace, joy and life for any relationship. This is the basis of our *electrifying* fellowship with the living God.

It should be briefly mentioned that faith is essential to all of life. We cannot act, think or know without faith. In a given day, we believe our car will start; the sun will come up in the east and set in the west; our homes will not collapse; food will be available to purchase; books will be in the library; water will come out of the faucet, and so on. It is normal to live by faith. This type of "basic" everyday religious faith demands more — all of us — than some type of rational argument or sensual high. This is the faith of which Paul speaks.

* * *

> But when the time had fully come, God sent forth his Son, born of woman, born under the law, to redeem those who were under the law, so that we might receive adoption as sons. And because you are sons, God has sent the Spirit of his Son into our hearts, crying, "Abba! Father!" (Galatians 4:4-5).

It was a common thought in Judaism and early Christianity that important historical events were fixed by the purposes of God (Mark 1:14; John 2:4; Acts 17:26). For Paul, God has His own time and His will is being worked out in accordance with His plan. It follows then that if this is true for the coming of Jesus Christ, it is true for the life of His followers, both as a body (the Church) and as individual members of that body. God's will for us is worked out in the fullness of time.

Jesus Christ had to come under certain conditions in order to put things right between God and humanity. He had to be "born of a woman, born under the law." He had to become incarnated. The manner in which He came is of the utmost importance. Without His life lived as we live, under the law and born of a woman, He would have

121

remained outside of our world of misery and alienation. But He came so that no area of human life or death was kept from Him. Born in Bethlehem, living in a family with parents, worshiping in the local synagogue and the Jerusalem temple, frequenting the streets and walkways of Jerusalem and His home village, meeting the bright and the limited, the healthy and the sick, Jesus became what we are fully and completely, in order that, as St. Athanasius says, we might become what He is — in right relationship with God the Father. Through Jesus Christ, God knows us well.

In this way, we are "redeemed" from the law. It is for this new freedom in Christ that Luther wrote, "The Epistle to the Galatians is my epistle; I have betrothed myself to it: it is my wife." Paul is referring to the Jewish law which held the people of Israel at a distance from God, a distance that preserved them from being consumed by God's holiness (read Galatians 3, where Paul discusses this fully; hence the law is a custodian, verse 24). Now Christ sets us free in that He completes the law (Matthew 5:17), or He fulfills the law for us.

Practically, this had enormous significance for the Pharisaic and legally trained Paul. Simply stated, it meant *no requirements*. The right relationship between God and His people, established in the Exodus events and contantly restated by the prophets, was established once and for all in the person Jesus Christ. And so Paul restates the prayer of the Pharisees which said, "Thank you, God, that I am not a Gentile, slave or a woman." He writes boldly to the Galatians: "There is neither Jew nor Greek, there is neither slave nor free, there is neither male nor female; for you are all one in Christ Jesus" (3:28).

For Paul, the logical results of this are profound! We now become the *children* of God. Inspired by the Holy

Spirit we can say intimately from the depths of our hearts, "*Father*" (verse 6). When life is depressing, worrisome, overwhelming, trying, we can cuddle up in prayer and whisper "*Father*," the most personal word in the Christian vocabulary. In Christ we are freed for God the Father — we are no longer slaves but heirs (verse 7). Paul goes on to write, "For freedom Christ has set us free; stand fast therefore, and do not submit again to a yoke of slavery" (5:1), that is, the slavery of the law. Bankrupt we stand before the Father with only Christ to claim. This truly is "faith working through love" (verse 6), the love of God that frees us for love.

* * *

> But the fruit of the Spirit is love, joy, peace, patience, kindness, goodness, faithfulness, gentleness, self-control; against such there is no law (Galatians 5:22-23).

The "fruit of the Spirit" could also be translated the "*harvest* of the Spirit." Paul argues that when we are free from the law, the Christian character is allowed to grow and mature and develop naturally in a living love-relationship with God through Jesus Christ and in the Holy Spirit. But the Apostle is not referring to spiritual gifts, as he does in 1 Corinthians 12:8-11 (see also chapter 4), where special endowments for special assignments in the kingdom are the theme. Here Paul wants to speak of the *natural* character of a Christian that reflects the divine life within. Perhaps we could even apply Augustine's description of a sacrament to Paul's "harvest of the Spirit": hence these characteristics are an "outward sign of an inward grace."

Notice, Paul is not referring here to the miraculous or sensational. These are not super-extraordinary expressions of divine power. Paul's statement reminds us of Jesus telling the parable of the seed growing secretly. The seed is scattered and slowly, surely and steadily the seed sprouts, grows and bears fruit and finally matures when "the harvest has come" (Mark 4:26-29). Again Jesus had taught, "for each tree is known by its own fruit. For figs are not gathered from thorns, nor are grapes picked from a bramble bush." Good is produced "out of the good treasure of [the] . . . heart" (Luke 6:44-45). Here is the peaceful growth of the Spirit's harvest. What an exciting thought that we are growing into a deeper and more mature relationship with God the Father.

Through "love, joy, peace," a Christian is empowered to face the mysteries and trials of life. These mysteries are the harvest of our relationship with the Father. The next five attitudes are directed toward one's neighbor (similar is the division of the Ten Commandments and the Lord's Prayer). Finally Paul mentions "self-control," a restatement that we must discipline and crucify "the flesh with its passions" (Galatians 5:24) so that Christ may live in us (2:20).

Paul then adds that "if we live by the Spirit, let us also walk by the Spirit" (5:25). The Spirit's governing of our daily living is a lifelong task. To crucify the flesh that Jesus Christ lives in us is not easy work. Especially in the area of social relationships, the Spirit must be our guide. For Paul, this primarily means the Church, the Christian fellowship. Hence through the Spirit's guidance, we should look for ways of helping and assisting one another.

* * *

Bear one another's burdens, and so fulfil the law of Christ. For each . . . will have to bear his own load (Galatians 6:2, 5).

Now we will look at the practical application of the Spirit's direction. When one in the fellowship of Christians falls, all of the members are involved (Galatians 6:1). This is the law of Christ, the law of love. The Jewish law perpetuated and encouraged individual achievement. Jesus Christ freed us from the law and taught that if one sheep is lost, a search for the one must ensue until it is found (Luke 15:1-7).

Yet the verses here seem to be in contradiction with what is stated previously. How can they be explained? The understanding of these verses is suggested in the Greek language. In verse 2 the sense is a burden that comes upon one with no clear explanation; a situation that happens with no rhyme or reason. A sickness, a death in the family, a handicap, an accident or injury, a growing old: "bear one another's burdens." In verse 5 the Greek suggests a backpack. This seems to indicate more the responsibility one "naturally" carries through life, similar perhaps to Paul's thorn in the flesh. Only oneself can shoulder and bear such a backpack. So Paul is saying, in effect, "Help each other when sudden problems arise and be responsible about your own accouterments."

* * *

Do not be deceived; God is not mocked,
for whatever a man sows, that he will also
reap (Galatians 6:7).

Here Paul presents a fundamental principle of the Christian life. This is an ancient proverb: one will reap what he sows. Paul is telling the Galatian churches that they must make no mistake: when God gives His Spirit, the receiver is expected to live by the Spirit. We must not live by the flesh but in the Spirit. Paul goes on to say, ". . . far be it from me to glory except in the cross of our

Lord Jesus Christ, by which the world has been crucified to me, and I to the world" (Galatians 6:14). The new values, the new priorities of Jesus Christ — of God's will — have been overcome or put to death in the Son's death on the cross. The new life in the Spirit is different from the life in the flesh.

But then again, do not think you can fool God. We cannot skirt the issue, we cannot avoid the truth. God cannot be hoodwinked, deceived or outwitted by false and insincere intentions. The wonderful gift of God's Spirit has revealed a new standard and motive-power for Christian living. Selfish ways and self-seeking motives are no longer compatible with the fellowship of the Spirit. So beware, God is not mocked. We cannot be lukewarm. Either we are with God or we are against Him (Revelation 3:16).

* * *

And let us not grow weary in well-doing, for in due season we shall reap, if we do not lose heart (Galatians 6:9).

Here Paul gives a caution to the Galatian congregations. This is perhaps the greatest danger to the Christian faith, the danger of tiring and turning to the selfish ways of rebellious unredeemed humanity. Jesus never wearied of warning the disciples about falling asleep in the faith. He constantly emphasized trusting in God (Matthew 6:25-34); watching (Luke 12:35-40); being faithful (Matthew 24:45-51); being prepared (Luke 14:15-24); being at work in the vineyard (Mark 12:1-12); readying for the wedding feast (Luke 14:15-24); keeping lamps burning (Matthew 15:1-13); employing talents (Luke 19:11-27). In the midst of all this, the disciples still "fell asleep." During the transfiguration (Luke 9:28-36), they slept rather than prayed and in the Garden of Gethsemane (Mark

14:32-42) the same thing occurs again. In the end they deserted Jesus, out of fear. Paul seems to be aware of all this as he cautions against the greatest temptation of all: growing weary in well-doing and therefore the faith (for there is no faith without well-doing!).

Again we notice Paul's emphasis that the spiritual life is one of slow lifelong growth and development. You are on a journey, says Paul, a spiritual maturing process that will continually bring you closer and closer to God until we shall see him "face to face" (1 Corinthians 13:12).

There will be hindrances, obstructions and delays. We may grow tired and thus ironically we may fall into evil ways by doing good! We may well tire of being helpful and supportive of people in the fellowship and so abandon the new inner life empowered by the very Spirit of God. So in verse 10, we could paraphrase Paul's exhortations: "As long as we have the opportunity, work at the good." The good life is a gift of God, but we must work at it if the harvest is to come — first in our own household and then in the household of God (Ephesians 2:19).

* * *

Henceforth let no man trouble me; for I bear on my body the marks of Jesus (Galatians 6:17).

What a way for Paul to conclude his epistle! He began by giving all the credit to Jesus Christ and now he ends in the same manner. He has struggled to vindicate his understanding of the Gospel of Christ and now he adds a very personal word. On his body he bears the marks, or the stigmata, of Jesus Christ. Paul is probably referring to the scars and wounds that he has received in proclaiming the message of the Gospel. Perhaps this is his way of understanding that he has been crucified with Christ

(Galatians 2:19) and has suffered physically (Colossians 1:24) for his service.

However the stigmata are understood, we can notice two things based on what Paul has said in his letter to the Galatian Churches.

First, the stigmata have a spiritual meaning. Paul's teachings on the Holy Spirit indicate that he understood all Christians as temples of God. Those who have taken up their cross and followed Him, like St. Paul, have the marks on their character through the harvest of the Spirit. So John Henry Newman could write, in "Verses on Various Occasions":

> *Yes! let the fragrant scars abide,*
> *Love-tokens in Thy stead,*
> *Faint shadows of the spear-pierced side*
> *And thorn-encompass'd head.*

Second, as a result the stigmata are a sign of ownership. Even the doubting Thomas recognized the Christ when he saw the wounds. Through the centuries it is no accident that many saints have borne the marks of the risen Jesus Christ on their bodies. For example, St. Francis of Assisi, in 1224, received the woundprints of Christ on his body. He appeared as having been crucified. Such is the *power* of the cross over our human nature or, as Paul says, when it is Christ who lives in us. Our ownership becomes a clear sign of the Christ who *lives* — and hence we live.

This sign of ownership is complete when we contemplate our Lord in the fullness of His Spirit. It is this concentration which makes a "new creation." All our knowledge, our experiences, our values, are radically changed as a new life of maturity begins moving slowly toward the harvest. This is the excitement of living in right relationship with a living God.

Paul's Letter to the Ephesians

Ephesus was the major city on the western side of Asia Minor. It was a seaport, heavily populated, and a great trading center. The ancient pre-Greek Ionian religion was based in Ephesus, a cult devoted to the Anatolian mother-goddess Artemis. The image of Artemis was in the temple at Ephesus; a stone image that fell from the sky, possibly meaning an image of divine workmanship (Acts 19:35). Paul was confronted with a riot in Ephesus because a silversmith named Demetrius organized a crowd of tradesman to protest Paul's many converts to Christianity. The loss of "Artemis believers" apparently caused an economic crisis for those "who made silver shrines of Artemis" (Acts 19:23-41). Not long before Paul's associations with Ephesus, the city was known as the "Temple Warden of Artemis" (see Acts 19:27).

Paul used Ephesus as a base of operations for three years during the third missionary journey (Acts 19:1-20). Paul had previously visited this city on his second missionary journey (Acts 18:19-21), and must have been familiar with at least a portion of the believers. During Paul's extended visit, he directs the proclamation of the Gospel to the Phrygian cities of Colossae, Laodicea and Hierapolis. The Good News was heard (Acts 19:10), and up until the twentieth century Ephesus had a thriving Christian community. It can be argued convincingly that this letter was written for all Christians in Phrygia and not just those in Ephesus. For example, among other arguments, there are no personal greetings, and the phrase "at Ephesus" in verse 1 is missing from the oldest manuscripts. Perhaps Ephesians is better understood as a "circular letter," an epistle to be passed around, as suggested in Colossians 4:16 with regard to a letter we no longer possess. (Some have argued that Ephesians is the letter mentioned in Colossians 4:16.)

Historical Context

Assuming Ephesians is probably a circular letter, it is difficult to reconstruct original settings. However, two general themes present themselves which may indicate the need for such an epistle. On the one hand, tension appears to have developed between Gentile Christians and Jewish Christians. Writing to the Galatians, Paul is concerned to deal with certain Judaizers who wanted Gentiles to become Jewish in order to be Christian. In cities with perhaps larger Gentile-believing communities, the problem is reversed. Now Gentile Christians need to be more accepting of Jewish Christians. Anti-Semitism developed early in Christianity and perhaps Ephesians is already addressing the problem.

On the other hand, there appears to have been some "gnostic" problems. (*Gnōsis* is the Greek term for knowledge or wisdom.) Similar to the theme in Colossae, Ephesians alludes to escaping from the body and ascending to a higher realm, "the spirit of your minds" (Ephesians 4:22-24). A further emphasis speaks of "licentiousness" and the practice of "uncleanness" (4:19). Several types of folk and mystery religions tended toward gnosticism. From several characteristics of gnosticism, the following are worth mentioning: (a) an unknowable transcendent God whose opposite is the god of the Old Testament, the god of the visible creation; (b) one's true "I" is a spark of deity; (c) a divine call awakens one to knowledge of the true self and God. These beliefs could easily dilute Paul's proclamation of the Gospel. Hence he writes with this in mind.

Summary of Contents

Paul begins with his "normal" starting point. Christ is central to the believer and to God's plan of salvation (Ephesians 1:1-10). Although the receivers of the letter had lived in the flesh, now they were new creations. Not only was Christ their savior but He is the source of all things in heaven (God) and on earth (humanity and creation). He is the basis for all spiritual, intellectual and divine understanding (Ephesians 1:11 and 3:21).

On the basis of these doctrinal statements, Paul adds ethical conclusions. Unity that is derived from Christ translates for all intents and practices as unity of faith. Be worthy of your calling, says Paul, and "maintain the unity of the Spirit in the bond of peace" (4:3). Turn away from the pagan life of the past and be united in church fellowship through the Holy Spirit (4:1-5:21).

Paul then encourages the believers to maintain a stable and sound social life. Make sure that your life is ruled by the principle of self-giving agape (love), whether on the job or in the home. There will be problems, there will be troubles, there will be resistance to the will of God, but stand firm and "put on the whole armor of God" (Ephesians 6:11). All this can only be accomplished in one way: stand firm in Christ. He is your strength, your purpose, your power against the evil one.

Paul ends his letter with reassuring words, directing the readers back to his starting point: "Grace be with all who love our Lord Jesus Christ with love undying" (Ephesians 6:24).

Passages for Everyday Living

For he has made known to us in all wisdom and insight the mystery of his will, according to his purpose which he set forth in Christ as a plan for the fulness of time, to unite all things in him, things in heaven and things on earth (Ephesians 1:9-10).

Here Paul expands the thinking of his readers. He is attempting to explain how Christ is *all* the wisdom and insight one can indeed bear. Everything has been made clear if we simply view life, the world, and especially God, through the prism of Christ. Prior to these verses, Paul tabulates believers' *assurances* offered in Christ: God "chose us in him before the foundation of the world" (Ephesians 1:4); he "destined us in love" to be His children (verse 5); this is "the purpose of his will" (verse 5); "In him we have redemption" and forgiveness (verse 7); these are the "riches of his grace" (verse 7).

These Christian assurances add up to the *mystery* of His will. God's will is made known and is being made known in Christ. This is a dynamic and constant occurrence. In Christ, through the Holy Spirit, a true fellowship with God has been established and now "all things" are united. This grand and difficult clue to the secrets of the universe is well portrayed in the Eucharist. The Greek word *mystērion* (mystery) was translated into the Latin as *sacramentum* and then to the English as sacrament. Hence, all "sacraments" are mysteries, that is, events that bring believers into an intense and intimate communion with the very will and purpose of God. Sacraments allow Christians to celebrate the fact that God is in control of the universe.

We can note several things about Paul's use of *mystery*, a term found in three of his letters: Colossians (four times), Corinthians (five times) and Ephesians (six times). It is also a term that captures well the theme of Paul's first thoughts for the Ephesian epistle.

(a) *Mystery* refers to God's intervention in history. He is present in history, yet can be encountered through faith alone. He gives himself to humanity, yet remains Lord of the universe. This is the essence of the *mystery*. In the Gospel of Mark, Jesus says to the Twelve Apostles: "To you has been given the secret of the kingdom of God, but for those outside everything is in parables; so that they may indeed see but not perceive, and may indeed hear but not understand. . ." (Mark 4:11-12). Accordingly, Paul speaks of the mystery of the cross (1 Corinthians 2:7); the mystery of Christ's presence in us (Colossians 1:27); the mystery of the Church (Ephesians 3:4); the mystery of proclaiming the Gospel (1 Corinthians 2:13-3:9); and the New Testament Book of Revelation speaks of the mystery of the second coming of Christ (chapters 17-22).

Mystery then is God's *choice*. God chooses to be hidden in His revelation; He chooses the weak things to confuse the strong; He has chosen time for eternity; He chooses flesh to reveal His spirit; He chooses humanity to reveal His divinity; He chose the cross to make known His strength; He has chosen the stammering person to speak His message. This is the mystery of which Paul speaks — the mystery of God's free choice to intervene in the life of creation in general and humanity in particular.

(b) The mystery of God's will remains unfinished. The future is yet to be completed. The final disclosure and fulfillment are "not yet." The secret of history, God's eternal wisdom and the truth of the prophetic message, is yet to be completed. This is the Christian hope (Romans 8:24-25), shrouded in mystery and held in faith (Hebrews 11:1). So Paul (quoting freely from Isaiah 64:4) reassures the Corinthian believers, "What no eye has seen, nor ear heard, nor the heart of man conceived, what God has prepared for those who love him" (1 Corinthians 2:9).

What a marvelous Pauline term, *mystery*! On the one hand, it means the wisdom of the Father's redemptive purpose executed in Christ through the Holy Spirit. Christians are called to participate in the very process of the Father's plan, God's coming kingdom. On the other hand, even though it is beyond our scope of comprehension, we can wonderfully, intimately and actively participate in the mystery, the essence of His will through the sacraments — especially the *Eucharist*. In this manner, according to Paul, believers are "sealed with the promised Holy Spirit, which is the guarantee of our inheritance until we acquire possession of it, to the praise of his glory" (Ephesians 1:13-14).

This is how Paul wonderfully stretches the minds of his readers, encouraging them to maturity in faith through Christ.

* * *

> ... the God of our Lord Jesus Christ, the Father of glory, may give you a spirit of wisdom and of revelation in the knowledge of him, having the eyes of your hearts enlightened. . . (Ephesians 1:17).

Paul is prayerfully concerned for these believers. He

is concerned that in the mystery of God's will, His grace will be sufficient for them regardless of circumstances. Paul is acutely aware that life is not easy. Having suffered much himself (2 Corinthians 11:16-33), He knows pain, sorrow and hardship. But notice how Paul is prayerfully concerned. He begins not with the difficulties of life, but with words of encouragement emanating from God. He is saying, in effect, "Do not get preoccupied with your own circumstances. Consider the Father and His grace first, then think on your own situation."

Twentieth-century religious thought does not always appreciate Paul's method. Due to a complexity of various theological and philosophical developments, we tend to think from one's self — whether internal or external self — to God. We tend to get very preoccupied with our own circumstances. Notice, however, how Paul proceeds. His starting point is always God in Christ. This is the true Christian assurance that assists the believer in dealing with every situation, every aspect of life. If God is God, how can we *believe* or *think* otherwise? The Christian must always *begin* with God and His love made known in Christ. This is Paul's perception of "a spirit of wisdom and of revelation in the knowledge of him" (Ephesians 1:17).

It would follow of course that Christ is brought into our situation. Paul proceeds to speak of how his readers were made alive in Christ (2:1) and dead to the world of sin. Paul begins with God's grace in Christ and carefully applies it to everyday circumstances. Of course, this is what the Church has struggled to do throughout history: apply God's grace to the lives of Christians. At a funeral, a baptism, an ordination, a counseling situation, a wedding, the grace of God is brought to bear upon everyday circumstances and situations. But it is God's grace that begins it all; that enters the human arena breaking into the marketplace of life with its healing, soothing, comforting, restoring, uplifting power. Hence the "eyes of your hearts" are enlightened.

* * *

For by grace you have been saved through faith; and this is not your own doing, it is the gift of God — not because of works, lest any man should boast. For we are his workmanship, created in Christ Jesus for good works, which God prepared beforehand, that we should walk in them (Ephesians 2:8-10).

These verses are the conclusion of a marvelous section. Paul wants to develop his main theme more clearly, that Christians are one in Christ, are forgiven in Christ and are set free for true living in Christ. In order to show how a person moves from *death* to *life*, Paul speaks in the past tense of being spiritually dead, disobedient and sinful (2:1). The new believers had been subject to the "spiritual powers in space" (see verse 2), living without principles or godly values. Paul gives us an amazingly clear description of life without God. Life without purpose, direction or meaning. Here is life on the dark side of existence.

In the midst of all this came God's love. Facing potential rejection of His self-giving love, God sent His Son to love us in our disobedience, while we were "spiritually dead" (see verse 5). What an amazing thought! No matter how often one hears this Good News from God's revelation, one can only contemplate and marvel over its depthless meaning and truth. John the Evangelist's words ring with clarity and truth: "The light shines in the darkness, and the darkness has not overcome it"

(John 1:5). Paul speaks of this "light" throughout this section in terms of grace, mercy, love, together with Christ, being saved by grace, God's kindness, the immeasurable riches of His grace. Paul leaves us without a doubt as to where the light comes from; it comes from outside us, outside our world, it comes literally from another dimension of existence, the existence of God's very being. Hence the Christian's life is "hid with Christ in God" (Colossians 3:3) making Christ's followers "a colony of heaven" (see Philippians 3:20).

We also must notice here Paul's tremendous statement about faith. The verses before us explain the origination and endurance of faith. The Christian is saved by faith, which "is the gift of God" (Ephesians 2:8). Works do not give us the preparation to see the light (verse 9). Only faith can allow us to penetrate the truth, and this is a gift from God. Not only does God act first, and on our behalf, but Paul now explains that He gives us faith to perceive what He has accomplished — a restored fellowship between God and ourselves. Faith is the means of appropriation. Believing demands our all, not just the mental side of our nature, or the emotional side, or the ethical side, or the spiritual side. Faith is God's call for us to respond to His mighty acts of love toward us, concentrated in the person Christ Jesus.

This origination of faith makes it durable indeed. It can endure anything and everything, even the dark moment of death and suffering. Faith has such endurance that it brings light to a person's darkest hour. Paul concludes this section about death and resurrection in his first Corinthian letter with a paraphrase from the Prophet Hosea (13:14): "O death, where is thy victory? O death, where is thy sting?" (1 Corinthians 15:55). Faith then is not something that we muster up and hold out for all the world to see. It is a gift! Faith is not something based upon our strength of will — it is free for the taking. This makes it durable and lasting — that is, divine in nature — if only we take and use it.

Jesus taught that faith is a gift from God that comes through the work of the Holy Spirit. "Every sin and blasphemy will be forgiven ... but the blasphemy against the Spirit will not be forgiven. And whoever says a word against the Son of man will be forgiven; but whoever speaks against the Holy Spirit will not be forgiven, either in this age or in the age to come" (Matthew 12:31-32). To speak against the Spirit, to blaspheme the Holy Spirit, is to reject the overtures, the inclinations, the beckonings of God calling us to himself, calling us home, calling us to have faith in Him. To not have faith, to go our own way, to pursue the truth somewhere else in this world is to "harden one's heart" against God and the Holy Spirit, a constant obstruction to those who would understand Jesus' teachings (for example, Mark 6:52, 8:17 and John 12:40). In a marvelous section, Paul writes later in this letter that the Father will strengthen them through the Spirit in the inner person, "that Christ may dwell in your hearts through faith ... that you may be filled with all the fulness of God" (Ephesians 3:17-19). This is the wonderful work of the Holy Spirit of God.

Paul does not stop with the acceptance of faith. He goes on to explain how Christians are God's workmanship, "created in Christ for good works" (verse 10). The Christian is not only beckoned to take up faith and believe in the healing power of Christ through the Spirit, but *now* one should live accordingly. One does not live and act in order to obtain faith — that would be earning God's love. Rather, faith is a gift that enables one to live differently. Confession in weekly worship reminds us of our need to live in accordance with what we believe, that God so loved the world that He gave His only Son.

* * *

*So then you are no longer strangers
and sojourners, but you are fellow citizens
with the saints and members of the household of God, built upon the foundation of
the apostles and prophets, Christ Jesus
himself being the cornerstone, in whom
the whole structure is joined together and
grows into a holy temple in the Lord; in
whom you also are built into it for a dwell-
ing place of God in the Spirit (Ephesians
2:19-22).*

Here Paul wonderfully states the unity of the Church
in Christ. The unity theme is a major emphasis in Paul's
letter, reflecting the struggles of the early Church, struggles that have not gone away. These verses stand as a
summary of what Paul has been saying thus far in his
epistle.

Christ cannot be reduced to a secondary position. Pa-
triotism, infighting, power struggles, ecclesiastical authority, even the authority of Scripture, have in the past
usurped the place of Christ and held His power and truth
in check. This was an obvious danger for those who were
about to receive Paul's letter. Christ must be central.
The Church owes its very existence to Him and it must
not misplace this truth.

Hence the Church is a commonwealth, the only truly
free kingdom on earth. Paul speaks here of the touchy
situation between Jews and Gentiles. Gentiles are no
longer strangers and foreigners, but are members of His
kingdom, joining the chosen people, the Jewish "saints."
This is the makeup of God's household, and it is the
place where He dwells (see 2 Corinthians 6:16). He is
the cornerstone, the one who makes it all happen. With-

out the cornerstone, there would be no building. Everything is welded together in Him. In Him, we are the temple of God. Paul's explanation brings to mind a verse from 1 Peter: ". . . like living stones be yourselves built into a spiritual house" (1 Peter 2:5). To be a member of God's household, God's commonwealth, Christ's Church, is to be alive and living out the gift of faith, acting accordingly. This is our call to be a living stone, intimately related to the cornerstone. Nothing can come in between the cornerstone and the other stones. Paul is quite clear on this matter. There is no room for negotiation. Christ is the center.

* * *

> There is one body and one Spirit, just as you were called to the one hope that belongs to your call, one Lord, one faith, one baptism, one God and Father of us all, who is above all and through all and in all. But grace was given to each of us according to the measure of Christ's gift (Ephesians 4:4-7).

Using a different figure of speech, Paul turns to ethical and practical implications. Paul appeals to his readers that they live a life worthy of their calling (Ephesians 4:1). After all, there is only one body, Spirit, hope, Lord, faith, baptism and Father. Here are the *seven* signs, or elements of unity, for the Church. These not only make the Church one body, but they indicate personal meaning to individual members. Paul states this in the seventh verse: each believer was given grace "according to the measure of Christ's gift."

Suddenly the Christian is called to responsibility. Christians are not simply free, but free to utilize God's grace for employment in the kingdom. We are not called to retirement. The Church is not a retirement village. Christians are called to action, to become living stones, to activate the spiritual gift bestowed upon each and every member. No one is left without a gift. Regardless of how small or large a gift, all are needed for the Church to be the Church. Paul implies that these gifts are only identified through a living relationship with God in Christ through the Holy Spirit. There is no idleness in the kingdom of God. There is no irresponsible living.

What are some of these gifts? Paul identifies a few when he writes, "And his gifts were that some should be apostles, some prophets, some evangelists, some pastors and teachers" (Ephesians 4:11). This could not have been a full list for the fledgling Church. Many other gifts were undoubtedly present, but these were the more important gifts that were critical for the spiritual health of the early community. We could add today gifts that have been important for the Church through the centuries. The gift of prayer, the long hours of prayer many practice that continues to be the umbilical cord of the Church. There is the gift of administration, implied in Paul's lists. There are the gifts of informal counseling, open confession, upbuilding, uplifting, compassion and concern for others, to name but a few. As the Church struggles to be the Church in the world, it needs all the many and various complex parts of its body. It needs all who accept the gift of faith and are given a gift to be used and traded in the marketplace of this world.

Paul implies two other things that we must note here.

First, the Church will never be a healthy Church unless all who receive the gift of faith live out their gift of grace. Paul speaks of "building up the body of Christ" (Ephesians 4:12). This is impossible without all the

141

members doing their part. Perhaps this is what plagues the Church today, a truth sensed by Paul so early in Christianity. *All* are called, *all* are commissioned, *all* have a responsible work to do, and the Church will always be less than the Church, unless *all* respond accordingly. The Jewish religion has a saying that if all Jews pray on three consecutive Sabbaths, the Messiah will come. Perhaps this is also a truth for Christianity.

Second, Paul also implies that Christians will never grow up in their faith unless they live their faith. Christianity is not a dead religion. One cannot expect to put his or her "faith" gift on the shelf and then revive it in the midst of a crisis. Paul goes on to speak here of "attaining" the knowledge of the Son of God, "to mature manhood, to the measure of the stature of the fulness of Christ; so that we may no longer be children, tossed to and fro and carried about with every wind of doctrine, by the cunning of men, by their craftiness in deceitful wiles" (Ephesians 4:13-14). He goes on to speak of how believers must "grow up in every way into him who is the head, into Christ" (Ephesians 4:15). If the Christian does not grow up and mature into the fullness of Christ, he or she will "grieve the Holy Spirit of God, in whom you were sealed for the day of redemption" (Ephesians 4:30).

For Paul, Christian maturity is a must. There is no standing still in the faith. Faith is a verb that implies action, movement, growth. If the Christian is not growing and moving forward, he or she is regressing, sleeping, falling into the darkness of unbelief. Perhaps Paul is speaking from his own life's experiences. Certainly his time in Damascus, the quiet years in Tarsus and then Antioch must have been years of growth, maturity and understanding of his new gift of faith.

For a believer not to grow up in the faith means

grave danger. There is first the danger of the individual, who may abandon his gift of faith in the midst of sorrow, pain, suffering and death for himself or for a loved one. Insight, knowledge and understanding about death and suffering do not come easily, but only through long periods of contemplation, as Thomas Merton has suggested; they come through devotion and fellowship with God as portrayed in the saints throughout history. Pain is evident in Paul himself when he mulls over his conflicting desire to be with God *and* his fledgling congregations (Philippians 1:21-24).

A greater loser of a dead faith is the Church. How can the Church be the Church unless all members live and act out their faith? How can a person be a member of a particular family and never live out that family membership? The Church of Christ suffers terribly for those who do not live out their faith. The body of Christ is wounded time and time again by those who would turn away from the responsibility of living out their faith. The wounds of Calvary on the person of Christ are intensified by immaturity and disregard for the precious gift of faith.

The greatest loser of all is God. He has loved the unlovable. He has given himself completely, taking no account of His own possible hurts by human rejection. He has, in His very being, willed to be in fellowship with humanity, the creation and the universe. So the obligations of the Christian to make a decision on the *Who* of Christ is always and everywhere present through the Holy Spirit, but not always recognized. Eventually a decision *must* be made, either yea or nay. Lukewarmness does not count. This momentous decision carries "eternal" meaning for one's self, the Church of Christ, and most importantly for a deity who has chosen us for himself and loves us regardless.

*Therefore be imitators of God, as
beloved children. And walk in love, as
Christ loved us and gave himself up for us,
a fragrant offering and sacrifice to God
(Ephesians 5:1-2).*

Paul's theme in this section is living out the gift of
faith. Paul has already established that we can know God
because of His light that shines in our darkness, that is,
Christ Jesus. Now we *must* be "imitators of God" because we know exactly what God is like. He is loving,
merciful, forgiving, kind, gracious — words often utilized
by Paul when speaking of God. In fact, Paul may well
have in mind Jesus' phrase about being "sons [or im-
itators] of your Father who is in heaven" (Matthew
5:45).

Paul then reverts to an Old Testament idea to explain Christ's life as a "fragrant offering" to God. The
meaning is that Christ's life was well pleasing to God. It
was an offering, a sacrifice, that gave God great joy, the
healing of a broken relationship between God the creator
and humanity, His creation. The Epistle to the Hebrews
takes up this theme very thoroughly, referring to Jesus
as the spearhead of a new community, One who has made
right sacrifice to God. The writer continues, "Let us run
with perseverance the race that is set before us, looking
to Jesus the pioneer and perfecter of our faith, who for
the joy that was set before him endured the [sacrifice of
the] cross" (Hebrews 12:1-2). This healing action is a
sweet fragrance to God and enables Christians to live accordingly.

Paul then turns to another figure of speech, that
wives be subject to their husbands (Ephesians 5:21ff).
Paul is not speaking in a vein conducive to modern-day

women's liberation movements, nor is he attempting to establish a family structure. He simply is stating in a new way the importance of keeping Christ as the head of the Church. The emphasis is not on the subjugation of women to men, but on the centrality of Christ for His Church. He is the husband and His wife is the Church. The analogy of Paul is drawn from life in the first century in order to emphasize Christ and His Church. It has no other meaning, with the exception of being a sociological commentary on the times. In fact, Paul carefully adds, ". . . let each one of you love his wife as himself, and let the wife see that she respects her husband" (Ephesians 5:33).

Paul ends this letter with a wonderful statement of putting on the full armor of God. Be an imitator of God, and *now* this can be done by taking the armor of the living and resurrected Christ (Ephesians 6:13-20). Gird "your loins with truth" he says; wear "the breastplate of righteousness"; put on "your feet . . . the gospel of peace"; take "the shield of faith"; wear "the helmet of salvation"; grasp "the sword of the Spirit," that is, "the word of God"; and "pray at all times." What a soldier Paul describes for us here! This "armor" needs careful meditation. One could paraphrase it thus: stand in the truth; keep your heart in righteousness; bring peace to where you go; trust the shield of faith; keep your vulnerable self protected with salvation; trust the Spirit through the Word; and pray always. Oh, that the Church were peopled with such a band of warriors! Surely His kingdom would come quickly! Paul concludes his Epistle to the Ephesians with a blessing of peace and grace (6:23).

Paul's Letter to the Philippians

The town of Philippi was well-known in the area of Macedonia, a province to the north of Athens on the Aegean Sea (Acts 16:12). The official language was Latin, and the town had a strong military history. Paul's Letter to the Philippians is unique because it was addressed to the first Church Paul established on "European" soil; and Paul and his companions were guided to Macedonia in a night vision, probably a dream (Acts 16:9-10).

Paul wrote the letter from prison (Philippians 1:7), but it is uncertain from which prison he wrote. He either penned the letter while imprisoned in Ephesus (early to mid 50s) or while imprisoned in Rome (possibly 55-58; or the more traditional dates, 60-62). *The Acts of Paul*, a gnostic Gospel that has not been given much influence, speaks of a further Ephesus imprisonment unrecorded in the Acts of the Apostles (also telling of Paul being miraculously delivered from lions in the Roman arena). But generally, the evidence is not clear. It can be concluded that the letter was written either from Ephesus about the year 55, or from Rome about 61 or 63. We will assume the latter.

Historical Context

Paul's purpose for writing to the Philippians was to thank them for their financial gift. They apparently had taken up a collection to assist Paul while he was in Rome. A member of the Church, Epaphroditus, brought the gift to Paul, helped Paul during his brief visit to Rome and carried Paul's letter back to the Church in Philippi.

Paul had approached Philippi in the usual manner, by way of the local Jewish community. It seems as though there were very few Jews in Philippi. Not only did Paul, Silas and Timothy remain "in this city some days" (Acts 16:12), but they went outside the city gates to a "place of prayer" by the riverside, a possible synonym for "synagogue" (although not for Luke). The first convert is Lydia, "a seller of purple goods, who was a worshiper of God" (Acts 16:14-15). She and her household were baptized, normally including slaves. This household probably became the basis of the Philippian Church.

Later some differences developed in the Church. There was conflict between two women in the congregation, Euodia and Syntyche. Paul eventually pleads, "I entreat Euodia and I entreat Syntyche to agree in the Lord" (Philippians 4:2). This perhaps is Paul's motivation in writing a section about not being selfish, ambitious and boastful. Paul concludes this section by quoting an early Christian hymn (2:6-11), most likely familiar lines to the Philippian Church.

There were some further problems within the Philippian community. In writing to the Thessalonians, Paul wrote: "You know how we had already been mistreated and insulted in Philippi before we came to you in Thessalonica" (see 1 Thessalonians 2:2). There was some type of tension with enemies (Philippians 1:28-30); there were those who would distort the Gospel by requiring other acts, perhaps circumcision (Philippians 3:2); and there were those who would preach the Gospel for wrong motives (Philippians 1:15-17).

Nevertheless, the relationship between Paul and the Philippian believers was strong and warm. The tone of the epistle is upbeat. Perhaps this healthy fellowship inspired Paul to point the Philippians in the direction of Christ's example. Paul only refers fellow believers to Christ's example on two occasions (Philippians and 2 Corinthians 8:9-10), a minimal amount, considering the great potential for instruction. Also, Paul does not rebuke the Philippian Christians. He does not speak of false doctrine, but emphasizes how he longs for them in Christ (Philippians 1:8), they being his crown and joy. His only warning is against disunity.

So Paul sends them back a letter after receiving their gifts. Epaphroditus is the bearer of this epistle.

Summary of Contents

Paul begins his letter with the normal salutation and thanksgiving (verses 1-11). He completes this section with an open prayer, asking God that "your love may abound," preparing the believers at Philippi for the day of Christ.

Paul then turns to his own circumstances. He tells of his imprisonment and how his struggles are for the sake of the Gospel. Even though there are false preachers who proclaim the Gospel for the wrong reasons, still the Gospel is proclaimed. He admits that life is a witness and labor to Christ, and that death would be a gain — and he cannot decide which he prefers (Philippians 1:20-24). In the end, he believes it best to remain in this life so he can help his fellow believers, the Philippians.

In the second chapter, he turns to the humility and sacrifice of Christ. Basically he says "stand firm" and follow Christ's example. (It is here that he offers the pre-Pauline hymn that tells much of the early Church's perception of Christ.) Following these encouraging lines of exhortation, he is inspired to tell of his own travel plans and how he hopes to send Timothy to them (Philippians 2:19-30).

The third chapter is a warning against compromising the Gospel: Do not allow persons to convince you that Christ is not enough. The practice of Jewish traditions will not help, regardless of what is said; nor will liberalizing tendencies that displace Christ the center. "Look at me," he says (see Philippians 3:17 and 4:1), "imitate me and trust only in the Lord Jesus Christ."

In the last chapter, Paul makes some final appeals for harmony (Philippians 4:2-9), gives hearty thanks for the gifts and the support Paul has received from the Philippian believers (4:10-20), and concludes with final greetings and a benediction (4:21-23).

Passages for Everyday Living

. . . I shall not be at all ashamed, but that with full courage now as always Christ will be honored in my body, whether by life or by death. For to me to live is Christ, and to die is gain. If it is to be life in the flesh, that means fruitful labor for me. Yet which I shall choose I cannot tell. I am hard pressed between the two. My desire is to depart and be with Christ, for that is far better (Philippians 1:20-23).

Here Paul pours out his heart, revealing his attitude and outlook on life. Shame can only come if he is not true and loyal to the living Christ. This is the one thing that is "eternally" shameful. In His suffering and even in His death, Christ must be proclaimed and testified. Hence Paul is determined not to be ashamed.

149

The most amazing thing is Paul's attitude toward death. Throughout history, humanity has feared death and its unknown character. Death is usually not something sought or even considered. Life is too sweet and good. Yet here is Paul torn between living and dying. Life for him *was* satisfying. It was rich and full. But "to live is Christ and to die is gain." What an odd outlook this must seem for people in the twentieth century!

Now Paul's Greek becomes a bit irregular. His mind seems to fly and move rapidly over future possibilities. If it were only his desire that had to be considered, he would literally "push off" and go to be with Christ. But his desire does not rule his life — Christ does. There is work to be done and he must get on with his assignment. Full and eternal fellowship with Christ must wait for a future time.

What an attitude Paul displays. Here is the wonderful and only Christian attitude toward death. Death is not the end, but the *gateway to real life*. Death leads to an immediate life in Christ. Assuming an "intermediate" state after death, the Christian goes to be with Christ immediately, but the body is not resurrected until the end of time. How else can we explain Paul's thoughts here? At death the Christian is ushered into a far better and greater dimension of existence than we currently know. Following Paul, the Christian pilgrimage in this life and in the world to come is centered in Christ. The living and resurrected Christ is the Christians' common denominator, the constant insurance, the never-changing assurance. So is Paul's dilemma about death: "To live is Christ, to die is gain."

* * *

Have this mind among yourselves,
which was in Christ Jesus, who [Paul now

quotes an early church hymn], though he was in the form of God, did not count equality with God a thing to be grasped, but emptied himself, taking the form of a servant, being born in the likeness of men. And being found in human form he humbled himself and became obedient unto death, even death on a cross. Therefore God has highly exalted him and bestowed on him the name which is above every name, that at the name of Jesus every knee should bow, in heaven and on earth and under the earth, and every tongue confess that Jesus Christ is Lord, to the glory of God the Father (Philippians 2:5-11).

Here is a brilliant early Church commentary on the person Christ. Although the author of the hymn is unknown, the theme is salvation and a secondary theme is Christian ethics. Another translation of the Greek in verse 5 would be, "have this disposition among yourselves." This is the attitude that Christ displayed. All Christians would do well to seek the same because His followers are the branches and He is the vine (John 15:1-10).

The hymn Paul now quotes summarizes Jesus' acts. Paul is concerned, it would seem, with what is done, with action. Christ did not develop an attitude in His followers by teaching them. He *acted*. In *His action*, Christians find an indication of a right attitude toward life. It is *because He acted* that we are freed to follow and act as He acted. He had to act first, and clear the way.

As the hymn indicates, Christ gave up all He had, all His preexistent splendor, to become incarnate, or "in the flesh," among humanity. He voluntarily entered the realm of death to rescue the dying. The hymn then turns to Christ's exaltation. He returns to heaven by way of the underworld. Now every knee above and below must bow, because He holds the means of salvation within His person. The hymn's content brings to mind Jesus' very strong statement that He is the door. According to John's Gospel, Jesus taught, "I am the door of the sheep. All who came before me are thieves and robbers; but the sheep did not heed them. I am the door; if any one enters by me, he will be saved, and will go in and out and find pasture. . . . The good shepherd lays down his life for the sheep" (John 10:7-11).

"Jesus is Lord" was an early Church confession. This confession was not just spoken, but was lived accordingly. As it was lived, it was a true action, a real and full witness and confession of Christ. During the times of Christian persecutions, when the Roman Empire treated believers so callously and cruelly, confession that Jesus was Lord could very well cost a person his life. But because Christ had descended to the creation from His place of preexistence with the Father, and ascended again to the right hand of the Father in order to plead the believer's case, the Christian was assured that death could not harm. Death was the gateway to life. Jesus was resurrected, enthroned, the Shepherd was awaiting His sheep. Or simply put, "Jesus is Lord!"

* * *

*. . . Work out your own salvation with
fear and trembling (Philippians 2:12).*

Paul offers some classic advice to the Philippian believers. Salvation for Paul is the fulfillment of the hope of the Gospel, the final blessing and full fellowship between God and humanity. Salvation is a gift, not something earned. But the believer must accept the gift and not passively wait for it to overwhelm.

Yet the emphasis is on "fear and trembling." All believers work out their own salvation, their living and ongoing relationship with the Father. So it was with Israel in the Old Testament and so it is with the new Israel in the New Testament. But Paul seems to be cautioning here that one not fall into spiritual complacency and self-satisfaction. The Christian must not think he can dilute the Gospel, pursuing one's own ambitions and goals apart from Christ. The Christian is dealing with *God*, the Lord of the universe, not some secondary authority. As one would not wish to make a mistake with certain individuals in business or private life, so one should not wish to make mistakes with God. Be careful to work out your salvation with fear and trembling, regardless of your station in life. This is a lifelong endeavor.

* * *

But whatever gain I had, I counted as loss for the sake of Christ. Indeed I count everything as loss because of the surpassing worth of knowing Christ Jesus my Lord. For his sake I have suffered the loss of all things, and count them as refuse, in order that I may gain Christ, and be found in him, not having a righteousness of my own . . . but that which is through faith in Christ . . . that I may know him and the power of his resurrection, and may share his sufferings, becoming like him in his death, that if possible I may attain the resurrection from the dead (Philippians 3:7-11).

What a true warrior is Paul! He is totally devoted to

Christ. Nothing can match the value of a living relationship with Christ. Paul speaks as one who had everything. He had Roman citizenship and all its privileges, he was a religious power in Jerusalem, he had sufficient possessions, he had self-confidence and pride in his person. He had all these things, but he lacked freedom for and with God. He lacked real freedom that is established by God's grace. He lacked the freedom of being a child of God. Now he knew true freedom, and nothing could match it. Now he knew God's possibilities, and not just his own limited and short-circuited possibilities. God's possibilities are limitless. God's possibilities for us are not restricted to plans, opportunities and lucky changes. Self-glorification and self-will have passed. The power of God was in Paul and he had done things in the service of Christ that would not have been possible from his old life of isolation from God.

Now through *faith* Paul was righteous before God. He was right with God because he trusted totally in Christ and did not rely upon his own good merit. Paul turns this faith toward the key factor, the resurrection of Christ. As he says on another occasion, "If Christ has not been raised, your faith is futile. . . . If for this life only we have hoped in Christ, we are of all men most to be pitied" (1 Corinthians 15:17-19). His resurrection and ascension back to the Father is the true anchor of every Christian believer.

But even more, Paul wants to become like Him. He wishes to suffer for Christ's sake, because of his joyous and glorious relationship with God through Christ in the Spirit. Nothing can match this fellowship. This is the essence of Paul's Christian theology. From this fellowship comes power, strength to experience the very sufferings of Christ and thus further binding and deepening fellowship and communion with God. Traditionally those close to God have sometimes born the stigma of Christ's sufferings on their body, and by experiencing His sufferings have drawn closer to Christ.

In this continual striving for deeper fellowship with Christ, death is no longer horrifying. If we share in His sufferings, we share in His resurrection. But the true basis for this motivation is a *fellowship of grace*. There is no earning of this fellowship. It is free for the taking — and deepening (1 Corinthians 15:54).

* * *

I press on toward the goal for the prize
of the upward call of God in Christ Jesus
(Philippians 3:14).

Paul is not interested in looking back, but only forward. Life is with the future, with the living that must be done, not with the past. He takes no pride in the past. He seeks only the prize of full fellowship and eternal rest with Christ. All Christians share this "upward" calling. As the Letter of Hebrews states, all "share in a heavenly call" (Hebrews 3:1; see also 1 Peter 5:10 and Ephesians 4:4). Each of us must press on toward the goal of full fellowship with Christ, becoming children of the Father.

* * *

But our commonwealth is in heaven,
and from it we await a Savior, the Lord
Jesus Christ, who will change our lowly
body to be like his glorious body, by the
power which enables him even to subject
all things to himself (Philippians 3:20-21).

After indicating that the enemies of the cross of Christ have the belly as their god, Paul turns to the Christian assurance. The Christian's homeland is in heaven. As a second-century *Epistle of Diognetus* states,

"Christians . . . inhabit the lands of their birth, but as temporary residents thereof. . . . They pass their days upon earth, but they hold citizenship in heaven." (See also Galatians 4:26; Hebrews 11:13, 16; 1 Peter 1:1 and 2:2). From this homeland the Savior, or Redeemer, will return to "renew" His followers.

This "new existence" of Christians will have something to do with the refashioning of bodies. Paul never attempts to describe the resurrected body, but he does speak of it in terms of an earthly body. He explains to the Christians at Corinth, "What is sown is perishable, what is raised is imperishable. It is sown in dishonor, it is raised in glory. It is sown in weakness, it is raised in power. It is sown a physical body, it is raised a spiritual body" (1 Corinthians 15:42-44). Paul is speaking of a "spiritual-physical" wholeness that will constitute the resurrected Christian — already made known in the resurrected Christ. This is the image the Christian is being transformed into, daily, through fellowship with Christ through the Spirit (see 2 Corinthians 3:18 and Romans 8:29, for example). As Paul states, "For now we see in a mirror dimly, but then face to face. Now I know in part; then I shall understand fully, even as I have been fully understood" (1 Corinthians 13:12).

Finally Paul offers some further appeals. He refers to the Philippians (4:1) as his joy and crown, and counsels: "Rejoice in the Lord always; again I will say, Rejoice. . . . Have no anxiety about anything, but in everything by prayer and supplication with thanksgiving let your requests be made known to God" (Philippians 4:4-6). What an appropriate way to end such a joyful and penetrating epistle!

CHAPTER SEVEN

Paul's Letter
to the Colossians

In four of Paul's letters, he refers to himself as a prisoner. Paul had been taken as a prisoner to Rome after his appeal to the emperor (Acts 25:1-12). Luke ends his Book of Acts with the statement that Paul lived "two whole years at his own expense" (Acts 28:30) in Rome. Paul had been under arrest, yet he "was allowed to stay by himself, with the soldier that guarded him" (Acts 28:16). During these two years, probably 60-62, Paul writes some letters to those who needed upbuilding and direction. The letters he dispatches are addressed to the Christians in Colossae, Philippi and Ephesus. Paul then writes a further personal letter to Philemon, who was a resident of Colossae. As a result, these four letters of Paul have been traditionally called his "prison epistles."

The city of Colossae was never visited by Paul (Colossians 2:1). It is located about one hundred miles from Ephesus in Asia Minor (present-day Turkey). Paul was resident in Ephesus for approximately three years and it is generally accepted that the Church in Colossae was founded by Christians from Ephesus who were trained by Paul. Epaphras, probably one of Paul's converts in Ephesus, was most likely the "missionary" to Colossae (Colossians 1:6-7; 2:1; 4:12-13). The Church in Colossae became a thriving community and indicates Paul's successful strategy, that is, establishing a central place of operations and reaching out to the surrounding communities.

Colossae was an industrial center situated on the Lycus River. Luke does not mention the three cities in the Lycus valley of western Asia Minor: Colossae, Laodicea and Hierapolis. However, it can be assumed that Ephesus was the base of operations for evangelizing these cities. We do know that Colossae had Gentile members of the Christian community (Colossians 1:27 and 2:13) and that a rather large Jewish population was relocated to that area in the second century B.C.

Historical Context

Paul received word about difficulties in the Church at Colossae. Epaphras came with a report to Rome informing Paul of exciting things that were happening at Colossae, but also of some wayward tendencies and acceptance of false teachings (Colossians 2:8, 16-23). Paul had learned of problems in Galatia and Corinth, and the "false teachings" of Colossae seem to include both of these previous heresies. In Galatia, Judaizers sought to combine Christian belief with Jewish belief, arguing that one must become Jewish in order to truly become Christian. In Corinth, an intellectual exclusivism threatened, which was a very common phenomenon in pagan cults of Paul's day. So Paul learns of a group in the Colossian Church who believed that Christ was not sufficient for salvation. They taught that faith in Christ must be accompanied by a secret knowledge of divine things and that this knowledge comes through some mystical experience.

One could get this special knowledge through certain

types of ritualistic services. These rituals seem to have centered around Jewish customs such as circumcision, dietary laws, Jewish festivals, and so forth. In fact, more emphasis is found in Paul's Letter to the Colossians on ascetic practices, or rigid disciplining of the flesh, than the explanation of Christian grace. This would indicate that Paul was told of imbalance that did not emphasize rigid legalism (as in the Galatian Church), but a type of enthusiastic moralism that watered down the Gospel of Christ — although, in the end, the same problem is evident in Galatia, Corinth and Colossae: *lack of trust in the sufficiency of Christ*. In Colossae, however, more complexities were evident.

These very early heresies encountered by Paul have never been absent from Christianity. In many ways it is the most difficult problem for believers. Paul makes his position quite clear when he writes to the Christians in Colossae, "Christ is all" (Colossians 3:11), therefore, nothing else is needed. But for the Christian, the greatest temptation is to dilute faith in Christ with other support mechanisms and assurances. Cardinal John Henry Newman once wrote: "Life passes, riches fly away, popularity is fickle, the senses decay, the world changes. One alone is true to us; One alone can be all things to us; One alone can supply our need." This is the essential message of Paul's Letter to the Colossian Christians in the Lycus valley, about the year 60.

Summary of Contents

After his normal salutations and thanksgiving, Paul wonderfully summarizes the supremacy of Christ. Nothing more is needed in the Christian life than Christ. He has accomplished everything, establishing humanity in a right relationship with God. Paul refutes the suggestion that Christ is only one possible manifestation of God, beautifully and succinctly stating that in Christ dwelt the fullness of the Godhead (Colossians 1:15-20).

After assuring the Colossians that he was truly interested in their spiritual well-being as a brother in Christ (Colossians 1:24-2:7), he again turns to the topic of false teachings. Apparently the Christians in Colossae wanted a deep experience in order to be assured of full salvation. Paul essentially agrees that they do need this deep mystical experience, but they could find it no other place than in simple truth of Christ living within them. In Christ are all the treasures and wisdom of life (Colossians 2:3). One has to trust in Him, living a life of mystical relationship with the resurrected Christ.

In chapter 3 Paul develops all the things a Christian has in Christ and the true characteristics and duties of the Christian life. He closes his letter with some messages and greetings (Colossians 4:7-18), ending with the words, "I, Paul, write this greeting with my own hand. Remember my fetters. Grace be with you."

Passages for Everyday Living

> We always thank God, the Father of our Lord Jesus Christ, when we pray for you, because we have heard of your faith in Christ Jesus and of the love which you have for all the saints . . . the gospel which has come to you, as indeed in the whole world it is bearing fruit and growing — so among yourselves. . . (Colossians 1:3-6).

In many ways, this is one of Paul's most impressive letters. Let us begin by noticing two things indicated in this passage. First, as Paul mentions in verse 7, the Co-

160

lossians had heard the Gospel from Epaphras, "a faithful minister of Christ on our behalf." Paul had never been to this rather insignificant city, had never met the Christian community members and now receives word that they were doing well *but* there was also some "straying" from the truth. What should he write? He begins with *encouragement*. Paul does not batter the Christian community with threats and warnings and intimidations. He does not begin by telling them they are wrong, their thinking is ridiculous, their attitudes are unfounded. No, he gently and softly encourages the Colossian Christians, "fanning" them in the direction of Christ. Paul is not preoccupied with his own authority and prominence in the early Church. He simply wants the Gospel of Christ to be lived and proclaimed. Hence his opening words are words of encouragement and upbuilding, having a very *positive* emphasis.

Second, Paul speaks of the Gospel growing and bearing fruit. Perhaps one of the most exciting and encouraging signs of the living Christ was the growing Church. As the "grace of God in truth" is heard and understood (verse 6), the body of Christ, the Church, surges forward as God's kingdom comes and His will is done. In various ages throughout the history of Christianity, when believers have been diligent about their faith, the Church has surged ahead. All Christians have the "input" to make this happen by their dedication, commitment, vigilance and prayer life. This was the excitement in the early Church, the leaps and bounds of growth and expansion. More and more individuals were excited and talking of the Christ who lives.

* * *

. . . We have not ceased to pray for you, asking that you may be filled with the

*knowledge of his will in all spiritual wis-
dom and understanding, to lead a life worthy of the Lord, fully pleasing to him,
bearing fruit in every good work and increasing in the knowledge of God (Colossians 1:9-10).*

Here is a wonderful summary of the Christian life of
faith. The key words are prayer, wisdom and understanding, life, bearing fruit and Christian growth. One thought
or word leads on to the other in Paul's mind. Prayer, that
constant access all Christians have to the very being of
God through Christ and the Holy Spirit, begins and sets
the pace of the Christian life. Without prayer there is little communication, sharing and assurance. We cannot
expect to maintain a "living relationship" with God if
conversation and communication with God are not constant and continuous. This is the "door" to the Christian
life of faith. But prayer is only the beginning.

Prayer, as conversation, gives access to God's will.
As in any relationship, communication makes known desires, wishes, interests and goals of the other party: for
Paul, "spiritual wisdom and understanding" come by
way of one being filled with the "knowledge of his will."
How to respond to a given situation, how to identify true
values in life, and how to perceive real issues, come
through knowing the Father's will and plan. "What does
God will for my life?" becomes the question that is an-
swered in and through prayer.

This leads to Christian maturity. As one grows in
Christian faith, everyday living patterns, habits and
choices are affected, and these "immediate directions"
lead to the eternal home. This is the life "worthy of the
Lord" which bears fruit, bringing His will to fulfillment
and completion. Where we walk, where we live each day

162

is influenced by the will of the Father, and the Father's will is to have fellowship with humanity. It follows then that God not only cares about our everyday living and the fruit or influence we have in our particular station of life, but that Christians should mature and grow up in His will, in a living relationship with the Father. This maturity leads to the eternal banquets with Christ in the heavens after this earthly life is completed.

All of this comes through *prayer*. Paul rarely fails to mention his prayers for others in his epistles. His prayers led to a clear perception of the Father's will for him and the Gospel. What Paul lived he encouraged in others. Ironically, one could not "become" that which Paul prayed without following Paul's example of prayer and communion with the Father. So Paul writes to the Corinthians, "I urge you, then, be imitators of me" (1 Corinthians 4:16) and "be imitators of me, as I am of Christ" (1 Corinthians 11:1; see also Ephesians 5:1; 1 Thessalonians 1:6 and 2:14).

* * *

He is the image of the invisible God, the first-born of all creation; for in him all things were created, in heaven and on earth, visible and invisible. . . . He is before all things, and in him all things hold together (Colossians 1:15-17).

Here is Paul stretching our minds to their fullest. Instead of attacking the "limited" thinking of some believers at Colossae, Paul takes a marvelously different approach. He puts Christ at the center of everything and broadens the picture so dramatically that the Colossians must have been struck by his breadth of thinking.

The false teachers in this particular community claimed superior knowledge of divine matters (Colossians 2:18) and emphasized certain rituals (Colossians 2:16-23). But Paul takes them to Christ. Here we have One who *is* the visible image of the invisible God. He alone is the clue to all reality — all things hold together in Him. The creation does not fly apart — because He *is* its rationale. In effect, Paul is saying, there is no knowledge outside of Christ. The superior knowledge that anyone would claim outside of Christ is impossible — and in the end includes such knowledge.

This is a critical passage for today. In an age when science and technology are part of life, when scientists search for the clue to the origin of the cosmos, when the universe continually and beautifully reveals its coherence and structure, Paul's thoughts must be taken seriously. Christ "is before all things, and in him all things hold together." If Christ is God, Paul's logic is faultless. There can be no secret or special knowledge, there can be no "private" wisdom that "adds" to the person Christ. Paul brings the false teacher's thinking directly under the umbrella of the person Christ. He is all in all. How difficult it is to stretch one's mind in order to contemplate such a truth!

Paul's statements bring to mind the opening verses of the Gospel of John. There the writer begins: "In the beginning was the Word, and the Word was with God, and the Word was God. He was in the beginning with God; all things were made through him, and without him was not anything made that was made. In him was life. . ." (John 1:1-4). This similarity of thought has led some to identify John's Gospel with Ephesus, the city from which Epaphras evangelized Colossae.

Throughout the history of the Christian faith, there has been a tendency toward the "security of spiritual knowledge." If one knows the Christian faith, if one has knowledge of Christ, if one possesses an understanding of

164

God, that is sufficient for a right relationship with God. Paul categorically and emphatically responds, *"No, that is not correct!"* Not only is knowledge of Christ needed, but a talking, living relationship must follow. How can there be love without relationship? "And what is more," says Paul, "Christ is so central and all inclusive, that He is the clue to all truth about God, ourselves (humanity) and the cosmos."

* * *

He is the head of the body, the church; he is the beginning, the first-born from the dead, that in everything he might be pre-eminent. For in him all the fulness of God was pleased to dwell, and through him to reconcile to himself all things, whether on earth or in heaven, making peace by the blood of his cross (Colossians 1:18-20).

What a statement of Christian joy! Some scholars have argued this to be part of an ancient Christian hymn. Here is Paul, writing from his prison cell in Rome, refusing to entertain an inflated view of his own importance for the fledgling Church. The head of the body is not himself (or another Apostle), the head is Christ — He in whom all things hold together. It was Christ who was raised from the dead. He is our *new beginning.* All followers of Him have new life because He lives. In fact, the whole of creation has a new beginning and a new life in Him. The Church is the beginning of a worldwide reconciliation, and the central principle is Christ. Again Paul "stretches" the minds of the Colossian Christians in order to put Christ in perspective and include logically *all* wisdom and truth under Him. This passage and the one prior demand long-term contemplation and meditation.

Then Paul indicates the trustworthiness of God's revelation in Christ. In Christ "all the fulness of God was pleased to dwell" (Colossians 1:19; see also Colossians 2:9 where Paul says again, "For in him all the fulness of God was pleased to dwell"). Negatively, Christ does not mislead. Christ does not misdirect. Christ does not give us one characteristic of God. Christ does not offer humanity a vague indication of God. Christ does not give us a shadow. Christ does not give us halfhearted assurance. No, in Christ "the fulness" of the living God freely dwelt. There is no distinction, no incoherence between *what God is in Christ and what He is in himself*. No other religion can make this claim. No other religion has such a stupendous truth — a person or incarnate truth. Paul states it simply and clearly — there is no need of anything else save the living and risen Jesus Christ.

Through His death comes *peace* between heaven and earth. Paul's statements remind us of Isaiah's description of the new heaven and the new earth. There he speaks of no more weeping, infant death or premature death, and there shall be pleasant habitats, enjoyable work and *continual conversation* with God. "The wolf and the lamb shall feed together, the lion shall eat straw like the ox; . . . they shall not hurt or destroy in all my holy mountain, says the Lord" (Isaiah 65:17-25). Paul bases this wonderful peace upon the cross of Christ. He who is the clue to the entire universe, died that sin be made harmless and so God's kingdom come. What a wonderful summary of Christian truth!

* * *

> . . . *Christ in you, the hope of glory.*
> *Him we proclaim, warning every man and*
> *teaching every man in all wisdom, that we*
> *may present every man mature in Christ*
> *(Colossians 1:27-28).*

Paul again addresses the essence of the Christian life. We need to note two important points he wishes to make: first, Christianity is not primarily knowledge, spiritual insight, a book, ascetic practices (Colossians 2:16, 20-23). Christianity is "Christ in you." Paul was radically changed because of his confrontation with the *living* Christ. On the one hand, the mystery of the Christian life is a living fellowship with God in Christ through the Holy Spirit that produces "Christ in you." Paul says in chapter 2, if you have received Christ, "live in him" (verse 6). Live in a way that is suitable to your Savior, but the motivation is because he lives and is in fellowship with Christian believers. On the other hand, the mystery Paul refers to in verse 27 implies the presence of Christ in the midst of all fellowships or churches throughout the Mediterranean world. Both individually and corporately, the mystery is "Christ in you" — this is the hope of glory, the hope of His coming kingdom.

Second, Paul goes on to speak of warnings, teachings and maturity. The mystery of Christ's presence implies movement, development and growth. Paul goes on to speak of being "rooted and built up in him and established in the faith" (verse 7). The metaphor refers to stability, but strangely a stability that comes from change, growth and maturity. There is no stability in standing still! Stability is maintained when one keeps moving in the Christian faith — sort of like riding a bicycle!

Paul of course does not mean avoiding the issues and keeping busy so as to not "question" one's faith. There is no attempt to escape embarrassment here. Rather, in faith, Paul says throw yourself completely and totally into the hands of Christ, and through continual conversational prayer — both explicit (words of address) and impicit (attitude), through teachings, through spiritual wisdom, *stability and security* will come through maturity.

Paul goes on to say, "See to it that no one makes a prey of you by philosophy and empty deceit, according to human tradition . . . and not according to Christ" (Colossians 2:8). Maturity and growth must occur in the Christian faith. Otherwise, philosophy, human theories, traditions of the past, and so forth will displace Christ and destroy faith. Growth or destruction are the only choices of the Christian — lukewarmness is unacceptable (Revelation 3:16). After noting the Colossian errors, Paul encourages them to hold fast to the "Head, from whom the whole body, nourished and knit together through its joints and ligaments, grows with a growth that is from God" (Colossians 2:19).

* * *

> *If then you have been raised with*
> *Christ, seek the things that are above,*
> *where Christ is, seated at the right hand of*
> *God. Set your minds on things that are*
> *above, not on things that are on earth. For*
> *you have died, and your life is hid with*
> *Christ in God. When Christ who is our life*
> *appears, then you also will appear with*
> *him in glory (Colossians 3:1-4).*

Christ is our victory over death and sin. After cataloging the errors of the Colossians in previous verses, Paul encourages them to seek the things above, where Christ now lives and dwells. Where is the living Lord? His lordship and complete victory are indicated in His position at the right hand of the Father. Because we are baptized in Him, we are also resurrected with Him. The things of earth can no longer have great and eternal significance. Christians must turn their thoughts to where Christ now lives — with the Father in heaven.

Paul is not speaking of escapism. In the verses that

follow, Paul is quite clear about things of earth and things of heaven. He lists the things of earth as immorality, impurity, passion, evil desire and idolatry, the things which are bringing the wrath of God. By putting away anger, wrath, slander, foul talk, one puts on the things of heaven such as love, compassion, kindness and meekness. This is not escapism, this is a change of values. Worldly things, like money, success, ambition, power, can no longer have meaning.

The Letter to the Hebrews, long thought to have been written by Paul, offers a vivid picture of the risen Christ. The writer speaks of the sanctuary of earth, the temple in Jerusalem, as the place where God dwelt. But the temple in Jerusalem was only a "type" of the real temple that is in the place where God dwells — heaven. Christ our sacrifice and high priest has ascended to the very presence of God with our "humanity" (but without sin) where He "has gone as a forerunner on our behalf, having become a high priest for ever. . ." (Hebrews 6:20). "Consequently," continues the writer of Hebrews, "he is able for all time to save those who draw near to God through him, since he always lives to make intercession for them" (7:25). As a result, a new covenant is established in Christ, allowing believers to seek "love and good works" (10:24).

This is the thinking of Paul. The Christian's life is hid with Christ in God because He lives and has taken our humanity to the very presence of the Father. Paul refers to the appearance of Christ, indicating his perception that the end time was near (1 Thessalonians 4:15; 1 Corinthians 15:51). He is glorified and we too shall be glorified for we shall be like Him, the firstborn, the new beginning, the new life. So Paul wrote to the Corinthian Church: "For now we see in a mirror dimly, but then face to face. Now I know in part; then I shall understand fully, even as I have been fully understood" (1 Corinthians 13:12).

* * *

> ... put on the new nature, which is
> being renewed in knowledge after the im-
> age of its creator. Here there cannot be
> Greek and Jew, circumcised and un-
> circumcised, barbarian, Scythian, slave,
> free man, but Christ is all, and in all (Co-
> lossians 3:10-11).

In the sections before and after these verses, Paul speaks of what the Christian life should and should not reflect. God's anger will be aroused by a person's life of "immorality, impurity, passion, evil desire, and covetousness, which is idolatry" (Colossians 3:5). Through the Colossians' baptism, the old life is broken. These are dark memories of their sordid past — and they must remain in the past. The old nature is now dissipated. Their heathen past is history.

Paul is quite clear why this old nature is "dead." It is not through any Herculean effort on the believer's part, but "Christ is all in all." Through the death of Christ, the principle of sin is destroyed. Then why do we sin? This is a problem that Paul and all Christians continually face. Why are we subject to passions that have been overcome by Christ's death? Paul offers two explanations to this dilemma and both are important.

Paul's one explanation is from the heavenly perspective. He indicates to the Rome churches that the higher spiritual life has not entirely arrived. The new life is present. Followers of Christ *are* new spiritual persons, but remain entangled with worldly matters. The flesh, as Paul states, still interferes with God's will. So Paul writes to the Rome Christians, "We ourselves, who have

170

the first fruits of the Spirit, groan inwardly as we wait for adoption as sons, the redemption of our bodies'' (Romans 8:23). We have the first installment, or advance, on the new life; we simply must be patient until it is fully realized. Hence we sin even though Christ destroyed sin with His death on the cross.

Paul's other means of explaining sin is from the believer's side. This is the explanation Paul uses in Colossians. He encourages the Christians to struggle and be worthy of their new condition. They now have a higher nature which ideally sets a standard of what is to be expected. The faithful must "work" at living this new ideal.

Sin then is overcome from two directions. God has come down to us in Christ, the "all in all" has led the way back to God. So we are now at peace with God, having a foretaste of full eternal fellowship. Sin is still around, but has been thoroughly defeated and will eventually be totally annihilated. This is our *hope*! (Romans 8:24-25; 1 Corinthians 2:9; 2 Corinthians 5:7; Hebrews 11:1). In the meantime, we must live accordingly. Christians must live up to their true self.

However, this is sought not in order to earn or merit God's love. The love (agape) of God is already a *fact* in Jesus Christ. The believer struggles to live the new life for two reasons: (a) in thankful response to the love God has shown toward us while we were yet sinners (Romans 5:8), or rebellious toward the creator; (b) so as not to inhibit or obstruct the coming kingdom of God. As Christ is all in all, so God is all in all. It is His kingdom that we pray to come, His will to be done and His name to be made holy. If our prayers are to be sincere, we *must live accordingly*.

The new nature evolves by being constantly renewed. Paul says believers are "renewed in knowledge after the image of its creator" (Colossians 3:10; see also 2 Corinthians 4:16). Through the new and living relationship between the Creator and the creature, opened by the life of Christ, continual knowledge of God's will conforms the adopted children more and more into the image of God. Paul does not mean that we become gods, but the life-giving relationship molds believers into true worshipers of God, that is, creatures of God. This is the true "station" or place of humanity. Then Paul lists the characteristic ideals of this new nature: holiness, agape (love), "compassion, kindness, lowliness, meekness, and patience" (Colossians 3:12), forbearing, forgiving, and peace in the heart. These characteristics reflect the content of Jesus' "sermon on the mount" in Matthew's Gospel (chapters 5-7).

* * *

Let the word of Christ dwell in you richly, as you teach and admonish one another in all wisdom, and as you sing psalms and hymns and spiritual songs with thankfulness in your hearts to God. And whatever you do, in word or deed, do everything in the name of the Lord Jesus, giving thanks to God the Father through him (Colossians 3:16-17).

One cannot be a Christian in a vacuum. Here is a brilliant description of the Church, the body of Christ. The Church is a fellowship that reflects *the* fellowship between Christ and a believer. The body of Christ requires that Christians help and mutually assist one another as God helps humanity in Christ through the Holy Spirit. This spiritual encouragement includes teaching and upbuilding one another in spiritual wisdom and the sharing of thankful song where appropriate. What an exquisite portrayal of Christ's bride!

The Christian's new nature is grounded in Christ. Therefore do all in His name. "Do everything for the glory of God!" writes Paul. In this way, all that is undertaken, whether in "word or deed," will not be a part of the old nature which seeks all things for self. A few verses down, Paul encourages: "Whatever your task, work heartily, as serving the Lord and not men . . . you are serving the Lord Christ" (Colossians 3:23-24). This is the believer's thankful response to never-ending life offered in Christ.

* * *

Wives, be subject to your husbands, as is fitting in the Lord. Husbands, love your wives, and do not be harsh with them. Children, obey your parents in everything, for this pleases the Lord. Fathers, do not provoke your children, lest they become discouraged. Slaves, obey in everything those who are your earthly masters. . . (Colossians 3:18-22).

Now Paul turns to the family. As noted earlier in Corinthians, Paul is indicating responsibility of all family members. He is not challenging the "system" but encouraging a sense of duty and accountability. It is as out of place to say Paul is encouraging the dominance of men over women as to say he is encouraging slavery. Neither is the primary concern of Paul. He is simply emphasizing the responsibility all have in the Christian household if all "words and deeds" are done in the name of Christ and for the glory of God.

Perhaps Paul was not challenging these structures because the end was near. To the Corinth Church he encourages everyone to "remain in the state in which" they were called. He goes on to say, "Were you a slave when called? Never mind . . . he who was called in the Lord as a slave is a freedman of the Lord" (1 Corinthians 7:20-22). Why this lack of concern for social change and justice? The new age was imminent. Paul concludes this section with these revealing words: ". . . deal with the world as though they [you] had no dealings with it. *For the form of this world is passing away*" (1 Corinthians 7:31; emphasis added). Structure was worth maintaining for the sake of proclaiming the Gospel. Perhaps today the opposite is true!

CHAPTER EIGHT

Paul's Letters to the Thessalonians

As noted earlier, some scholars argue that this was the first letter written by Paul (that is, 1 Thessalonians; some scholars argue that Paul did not author 2 Thessalonians). Its chronological place in the Pauline corpus of epistles depends upon where Paul traveled in Galatia (Asia Minor or present-day Turkey) during his first two missionary journeys. As a result, either Paul wrote Galatians at his first "ministry in writing" or he wrote 1 Thessalonians which was later followed by Galatians. But in the end, which letter was his first epistle is of secondary importance. We must simply examine the letters in the manner they have come down through history: as Paul's letters to Christians at Thessalonica.

Historical Context

Thessalonica was the capital of Macedonia. The city is to the north of Athens on the Aegean Sea and was an important port city. In Paul's time, it was very cosmopolitan and had quite a large Jewish population. Like Corinth, this would have been an exciting place to live and it would have offered a host of religious perspectives and cults. The fact that some of Paul's followers were taken before the "city authorities" (Acts 17:6) indicates a free city with its own local political system.

According to Luke, Paul and his followers were on their second missionary journey. They traveled through Asia Minor but were forbidden by the Holy Spirit to speak the Gospel (Acts 16:6). Not being guided by God to travel north (to Bithynia, Acts 16:7-8), eventually some direction is received. Luke tells of how Paul had a vision (or a dream), and in the vision "a man of Macedonia was standing beseeching him and saying, 'Come over to Macedonia and help us.' And when he had seen the vision, immediately we sought to go on into Macedonia, concluding that God had called us to preach the gospel to them" (Acts 16:9-10). How clearly Paul and the early Christians understood themselves guided by the Spirit of God!

After sailing for Troas (Acts 16:11-12), they traveled to Philippi in Macedonia. After some missionary work, Paul and Silas are flogged and thrown into prison. Exercising his rights as a Roman citizen, Paul demands an apology and then travels east about one hundred miles to the city of Thessalonica. Meanwhile, Luke, one of Paul's traveling companions, stayed in Philippi to shepherd the new Christians. Paul, Silas and Timothy arrive in Thessalonica about the year 50 (Acts 16:22-17:1).

Paul went to the synagogue, "as was his custom" (Acts 17:2). He discussed and argued over the Scriptures (the Jewish Scriptures), with the result that some became believers and some became very hostile. Paul's essential message was: "This Jesus, whom I proclaim to you, is the Christ" (Acts 17:3). Those who became believers were Jews (see Acts 17:10 where Luke suggests that the Jews in Thessalonica were not very "noble"), "many of the devout Greeks and not a few of the leading women" (Acts 17:4). Because of the hostility, Paul and his companions stayed only three weeks (or three Sabbaths), departing in the middle of the night and traveling to the city of Beroea east of Thessalonica (Acts 17:10). But even in Beroea, Jews from Thessalonica arrived to stir up the crowds against them (Acts 17:13). Once again Paul is hastened out of the city by the brethren, traveling to Athens where he engages Jews in the synagogues and the Greek philosophers at the Areopagus. Meanwhile, Silas and Timothy remained in Beroea to assist the new Christian community (Acts 17:14-34).

It is worth noting that Luke refers to "the house of Jason" as the center of Christian activity in Thessalonica. It was Paul's practice to take up residence in the homes of individuals (Lydia, Acts 16:13-15; Priscilla and Aquila, Acts 18:2; Titius Justus, Acts 18:7). These households appear to be basic units for establishing and developing the early Church. Early Christian worship was held in private homes, households which included immediate family members, relatives, slaves, freedmen, hired workers, tenants and sometimes even business partners (see Romans 16:14; also 1 Corinthians 1:11, 16; 11:20, 34; 14:23; Philippians 4:22; Colossians 4:15). The basic importance of the family unit brings advantages and disadvantages to the early Church, evidenced, for example, in Paul's attempt to deal with factions within households (1 Corinthians 1-4). But regardless, the Christian household or house church remains vital to "the household of God."

After Paul's visit to Athens, he travels to Corinth. Silas and Timothy rejoin Paul in Corinth and tell him of the situation in Thessalonica. During a period of six months, the Christians had been true to their calling in Christ and as a result the message of Jesus had spread throughout the region. However, there were some problems: the Jews were hostile; there was possibly a persecution; there was some concern about sexual im-

177

morality; there was a concern over Church leadership; and there was concern about the state of Christians who died. Paul responds to this news with a letter, 1 Thessalonians.

Within a few months, further problems developed. Questions of God's faithfulness, more discussions on the state of Christians who died and questions about the expected return of Jesus prompted Paul to write again. So he wrote 2 Thessalonians, which is an attempt to correct some of the misunderstandings of his first letter.

Summary of Contents

Paul's preaching of the Gospel "in the Holy Spirit" (1 Thessalonians 1:5) established his initial relationship with the Thessalonians. Afterward, Paul and his companions labored "night and day" (1, 2:9 and 2, 3:7-8) to support their stay with the Thessalonians. They proclaimed and taught the Gospel of Christ and were eventually forced to leave the city (1 Thessalonians 2:15). But Paul's concern for the new Christian community was great. Because he was unable to return and visit with them (2:17-20), he sent Timothy to encourage the community (chapter 3). Timothy returns, joining Paul in Corinth and dispatches good news of their faith and bad news of some conflicts.

Paul was accused of personal gain in his preaching. Furthermore, some members of the new community were weak, fainthearted, questioning the status of those deceased and questioning the second coming of Christ. Paul deals with these issues in chapters 4 and 5.

Generally, this is a positive letter, upbeat and full of assurance. Paul attempts to comfort and encourage those who heard his initial proclamations. Here we find Paul the Apostle concerned for the pastoral care of the new Christians in Thessalonica. Hence the idle are to work, the fainthearted are encouraged in the faith, teachers must be responsible in teaching and all must "encourage one another and build one another up" (1 Thessalonians 5:11).

The second letter is brief and follows soon after the first. Paul simply reiterates part of what was stated in the first correspondence. His concern is to remind the Thessalonians that the judgment of God will come (chapter 1), that Christ will return — so be patient (chapter 2), and do not hesitate to work (chapter 3).

Passages for Everyday Living

We give thanks to God always for you all, constantly mentioning you in our prayers, remembering before our God and Father your work of faith and labor of love and steadfastness of hope in our Lord Jesus Christ (1 Thessalonians 1:2-3).

Paul's thanksgiving is directed to God. He does not thank the Thessalonians for their acceptance of the Gospel. For Paul, their acceptance of faith is made possible by God's gift of grace. So Paul directs his thanks to the source of all life and faith. But he does not stop with simple thanksgiving. He prays. He prays for the new Christians at Thessalonica, because he knows they are new babes in the faith, liable to be misled, misguided and misdirected. Their new faith puts them in danger. So Paul eventually states, ". . . I sent that I might know your faith, for fear that somehow the tempter had tempted you and that our labor would be in vain" (1 Thessalonians 3:5).

All Christians not only experience such an initial danger, but the danger is ongoing. Believers are constantly threatened by misunderstandings of God — perhaps that is why Paul directs his thanks to God. It is from God we turn and to God we return. The danger is that in our adoption as children of the Father we again rebel and turn from God. But Paul's remedy is sure: *constant prayer*. The gravest danger is that Christians become so self-assured that they forget prayer. Paul implies that continual prayer is the essential ingredient for the Christian life. For himself and the Thessalonians, constant prayer surmounts all dangers, problems and difficulties of the Christian faith.

Then Paul speaks of *the* three graces of the Christian life.

First, he refers to the Thessalonians' "work of faith." It is universally true that actions speak louder than words. Here the emphasis is on a person's faith that works itself out in everyday living, that is, in the marketplace of life. "Faith is of no value without works," says Paul. Do not bother with faith if you do not wish to live out the same in everyday life. On the other hand, Christian works are inspired by faith in God. Trust in Him is the inspiration for living.

Second, Paul then refers to their "labor of love." Here is the laborious toil that every Christian is called to live out. For whom does the Christian labor? We labor for others, giving of ourselves, responding to the needs of those whom we meet on life's way. Paul's words are energetic. Love is zeal, a sacrificial giving of ourselves. Christians must not shrink from the needs of those they meet each day.

Third, Paul then refers to a "steadfastness of hope" in Christ. Here is not meant a passive acceptance of life, a type of Christian patience. Rather, the Greek indicates a heroic endurance. This strong endurance is a virtue that the Christian believer relies upon to face the difficulties of life. The world is full of problems and the Christian is not immune from them, but is able to see beyond to the Christ. With Christ's resurrection the Christian moves out of the darkness into the dawn of a new age, a new time, a new life. This is the tremendous strength of the Christian hope, the hope that upheld the early Christian martyrs before the lion's savage attack.

The Christian graces for Paul are clear — faith, hope and love. For the appearance of these in the Thessalonian believers he gives thanks and prayers for their continuance. They became imitators of him and his fellow workers, and so "became an example to all the believers in Macedonia and in Achaia" (1 Thessalonians 1:7).

* * *

Finally, brethren, we beseech and exhort you in the Lord Jesus, that as you learned from us how you ought to live and to please God, just as you are doing, you do so more and more. For you know what instructions we gave you through the Lord Jesus (1 Thessalonians 4:1-2).

God does not leave us alone. Christians in the early Church felt assured that God's plan was being worked out and a Christian's needs would be supplied. Here Paul states how by grace he and his companions were an example for the Thessalonians. God sent a guide, a missionary, one who could tutor them in the faith. Through example and instruction, God does not leave us alone. Every Christian — even those in the worldly atmosphere and religiously synchronistic culture of Thessalonica, is provided with guidance, fellowship and communion. Because of the costly death of God's Son, abandonment is unthinkable!

In several verses that follow, Paul gives explicit instruction for Christian living. Because the city of Thessalonica was a very secular city and because the Christian community was newly established, Paul encourages sexual purity. He emphasizes things that to this day pose a threat to the marriage contract. He inspires the new Christians to "abstain from immorality" (verse 3), to take a wife in "holiness and honor" (verse 4), and to refrain from "the passion of lust" (verse 5). To do otherwise is to literally disregard God (verse 8).

Paul connects "sanctification" (verse 3) with God's call to "holiness" (verse 7). Sanctification, or holiness, is the result of action by the Spirit of God upon those who accept the gift of faith. This influence is incomparable coming from beyond the realm of humanity and creation, that is, from the Creator himself (1 Corinthians 6:19; Ephesians 2:19; Romans 15:16; and others). Hence the renovation of our character and person is not comparable to any other thing. Paul is quite clear that this is an action from God to humanity and it is not an isolated or once-only occurrence. It is a continual influence, a dynamic and ever moving wind that constantly inspires, revivifies, enhances and stimulates the Christian life. Not responding to this moving, energizing Spirit of God is to "disregard God" (see verse 8), the Father who will not let His children alone.

So to be sanctified is to be in a right and dynamic relationship with God. Saintliness is not a classification but a way of "life" — true life. In the Old Testament, this sanctification process takes primarily the form of worship. As the elected Jewish nation gathers in a holy place they sanctify and dedicate themselves to the *service* of God. Paul perhaps has just this in mind as he instructs the Christians in Thessalonica to please God, "for this is the will of God, your sanctification" (1 Thessalonians

4:3). Through a Christian's weekly worship and everyday service of God, one is drawn more completely and more fully into right relationship with God and is sanctified by the will of God.

* * *

> *But we would not have you ignorant, brethren, concerning those who are asleep, that you may not grieve as others do who have no hope. For since we believe that Jesus died and rose again, even so, through Jesus, God will bring with him those who have fallen asleep . . . we who are alive, who are left until the coming of the Lord, shall not precede those who have fallen asleep (1 Thessalonians 4:13-15).*

The Christians in Thessalonica were expecting the end of the world very soon. This reserve hope has appeared at various times throughout the history of the Christian faith. It appears that the unique aspect of the Thessalonians' future hope was their uncertainty about those already dead. Will those who have passed on share in the second coming of Christ? Paul's response is that *all* will share in one glory.

The pagan view of life was bleak indeed. The various philosophies of Paul's day spoke of hopelessness, despair, forlornness and death. There was no future life; there was nothing but an eternal sleep after this life was finished. One was powerless in the face of the chariot of death. Pagan funerals in the Roman Empire were held at night when no one could see this evil omen. (After the persecutions of Christians subsided, the Church chose daytime burial with a procession, and following Jewish custom made the burial of the dead an occasion for joy.)

One pagan epitaph that exemplifies the Roman attitude toward death, read, "I was not; I became; I am not; I care not."

But in Christ this despair is shattered. He lives! Because He lives, death no longer has any power over those in Christ. Paul does not suggest that death will not intrude upon life and claim its victim, but this type of "physical only" death is in the end harmless. The greatest miracle for Paul is that a person lives and dies in Christ, then even though the person is dead, he or she still *lives in Christ* and will rise with Christ. The living relationship between the risen Christ and the believer is so strong and complete that death can do it no harm. Time cannot affect this relationship — a relationship that transcends all dimensions of existence. Nothing can separate us from this love relationship that holds us in our very existence.

Following the teachings of Jesus, Paul does not know the time of the Lord's coming (Matthew 24:36, 43). He does refer to us "who are alive" (1 Thessalonians 4:17), indicating his expectation and hope of being alive when the Lord returns. Drawing from his Jewish background, Paul paints a rather vivid picture of the descending Lord speaking out, the archangel calling, the trumpet sounding and the clouds accompanying God's action. Certain Jewish groups expected these things when God would come in glory to establish His kingdom on earth. Paul makes use of this imagery, in a very poetic way, to emphasize that "we shall always be with the Lord" (verse 17). What a marvelous way of stating the Christian's expectation of the future, a future based upon the living and resurrected Christ who will come again! This future occurrence can be "tasted" and experienced *now* because of the Christian's call to a wholesome and dynamic relationship with a living, loving and eternal God.

* * *

For you yourselves know well that the day of the Lord will come like a thief in the night. When people say, "There is peace and security," then sudden destruction will come. . . . But you are not in darkness, brethren, for that day to surprise you like a thief (1 Thessalonians 5:2-4).

The "day of the Lord" is an Old Testament idea (Amos 5:18; Joel 2:1; Zephariah 1:17; Isaiah 22:5 and 13:9; Jeremiah 30:7; Malachi 4:1; and others).

But Paul cleanly shifts gears from low to high, from the old covenant to the new covenant, from the day of the Lord to the second coming of Jesus. The Jewish expectation of God's coming emphasized its suddenness and abruptness, its universal upheaval and a final judgment. Speculation about this "day" was evident among Jews and Christians. And of course, Christians who experienced the hatred of the Roman Empire's persecutions did not hesitate to anticipate "God's end." Paul has two things to say about this day of the Lord.

First, no one should be caught unawares. Christians live in the light (1 Thessalonians 5:5), the light of God's word spoken to us in Christ. This eternal light "shines in the darkness, and the darkness has not overcome it" (John 1:5). If the Church, the body of Christ, and all its members cling to the light, trusting in the God who lives, trusting in the wonderful relationship of agape (love) between the Creator and the creature, they will be ready. No one who lives in the light will be delinquent. Paul, following his Master, encourages the Thessalonians to keep their lamps burning (Matthew 25:1-13), be ready (Matthew 24:36-44), be faithful (Matthew 24:45) and keep busy with their talents (Matthew 25:14-30).

185

Second, no one knows when the Lord will return or when our years will end. God will call us home, often without warning. Preparation has to be done prior to that moment. Paul seems to say the best preparation is to always seek the light and keep busy in the work of the kingdom of the light. Cling to the light and keep busy. An elderly gentleman was once asked about death, and his response was this: "A person is immortal until his work is done." All are under assignment from God and must keep busy with the work of the kingdom. In this manner, not only do we cling to the light but we can never be caught unawares by slipping idly into the darkness.

Paul ends his first letter with wonderful advice for the Christian. Here we have a *necessary* prescription for practical Christian health and well-being. Here is the sum total of the Christian life. These "end notes" demand prayerful contemplation and careful application. We can summarize them in this manner: "Be at peace among yourselves. Admonish the idle, encourage the fainthearted, help the weak. Always seek to do good to one another. Rejoice always, pray constantly, give thanks in all circumstances. Do not quench the Spirit, test everything, hold fast to the good, abstain from every form of evil. And may God sanctify you wholly" (see 1 Thessalonians 5:13-23).

Paul's Second Letter to the Thessalonians

We are bound to give thanks to God always for you, brethren, as is fitting, because your faith is growing abundantly, and the love of every one of you for one another is increasing . . . we ourselves boast of you in the churches of God for steadfastness and faith (2 Thessalonians 1:3-4).

Paul had apparently received a message from the Thessalonians. Self-doubting and self-questioning was evident. The Thessalonians lacked self-assurance that they were the Church, or body of Christ. Here Paul the pastor is superb in dealing with their doubts and misgivings. We must notice two important things.

First, spiritual growth, like any other type of growth, does not come easily. Growth is always accompanied by a period of adjustment and change. In the end this is inevitable, healthy and necessary. The required effort and dedication for increase pays grand dividends, but there may be periods of time when it will appear that no progress is being made — only ensuing chaos. In the midst of this congregation's struggles, Paul sees clearly. "Your faith is growing" and your fellowship of love is increasing (2 Thessalonians 1:3). What often may *seem* like a step backward is in fact true spiritual growth!

Even when Paul mentions their afflictions and persecutions, he indicates that all is well in the kingdom, for God shall "be glorified in his saints" (2 Thessalonians 1:10). In fact, he gives us the perfect example of how Christians should help, encourage and console each other during the course of each person's spiritual journey. Fellowship means caring and encouraging others, the exact opposite of the world's values.

Second, Paul turns the Thessalonians first to God and then to one another. Faith precedes the love of one another. A right relationship with God is the basis of right relationships with fellow humans. To confuse this starting point is to base one's life on something other than the Gospel of Jesus Christ. Paul in effect says do not despise yourself, rather love God and support one another. Martin Luther stated the same when he wrote, "Faith, like light, should always be simple and unbending; while love, like warmth, should beam forth on every side, and bend to every necessity of our brethren." Here are the marks of Christ's Church, the marks that will make you endure.

* * *

Now concerning the coming of our Lord Jesus Christ and our assembling to meet him, we beg you, brethren, not to be quickly shaken in mind or excited, either by spirit or by word, or by letter purporting to be from us, to the effect that the day of the Lord has come (2 Thessalonians 2:1-2).

This entire passage is very difficult (verses 1-12). Paul speaks of imagery concerning the end time in an attempt to instruct the Thessalonians. We cannot be sure of the things Paul told them when he was with them (verse 5), but here he is saying "keep calm." Do not get hysterical about the end time. They must have misunderstood Paul because he certainly did not mean to imply that the end had already come. In fact, several things had yet to happen; there had to be an age of rebellion, a revealed evil one and then would come a cosmic battle between evil and the Christ. (The reference in verse 8 that "Jesus will slay him with the breath of his mouth and destroy him by his appearing and his coming" is a possible reference to the Holy Spirit.) These are not unusual beliefs in the eastern world, and the picture Paul paints carries some truth for Christians today.

Evil is a clear reality in the world today. It rests essentially on a misunderstanding or rejection of God's will. In the end, evil is the rejection of God's rule over the universe. Within persons, it takes the form of the individual's desire to control his or her own destiny. They refuse to allow God any power in their lives and either re-

ject His will outright or distort His will in order to subject it to their own will (hence is the story of the fallen
angel). The clear result is the presence of evil in the
world, or, as the New Testament states, the anti-Christ
who wills the opposite of the Father (1 John 2:18 and 1
John 4:3).

However, *God's will* will prevail. Chaos may seem
to be all around us, resistance on every side, but even evil
is in the control of God. In the final battle, the Lawless
One will be overcome by the triumphant will of God the
Father.

* * *

*If any one will not work, let him not
eat. For we hear that some of you are living in idleness, mere busybodies, not
doing any work (2 Thessalonians 3:10-11).*

Apparently some individuals became lethargic and
unwilling to work. They were waiting for the second coming of Jesus. The Greek word Paul uses literally means
"to be absent." In other words, some in Thessalonica
were not accepting their responsibilities of duty and
work as members of the Christian Church. After referring to his own example, Paul indicates that if one is
thoroughly immersed in his own calling as a member of
the body of Christ, he will not have time to be busy with
the affairs of others.

In Jewish eyes, work was a blessing from God. The
Talmud, an early Jewish commentary on the Torah, or
law, says the following: "Greater even than the pious
man is he who eats that which is the fruit of his own toil;
for Scripture declares him twice-blessed." Even today,
work is considered the greatest contributor to longevity.
But Paul here speaks of spiritual health and longevity. If
a Christian is to grow and mature in the faith, work is a

189

necessary part of one's calling. Here lies the secret to spiritual sanctity, for even in our relationship with God all is established by His *acting* on behalf of the creature.

Then Paul picks up the quill and writes a greeting with his own hand. "This," he writes, "is the mark in every letter of mine; it is the way I write. The grace of our Lord Jesus Christ be with you all" (2 Thessalonians 3:17-18).

CHAPTER NINE

Paul's Letter
to Philemon

Philemon is the shortest letter in the New Testament, only twenty-five verses. It constitutes the only personal letter of Paul that has survived. It was probably written while Paul was under house arrest in Rome (Acts 28:39), sometime during the years 61-63.

Historical Context

Slavery was a necessary part of the Roman social order. Anyone who interfered with this social institution was in danger of severe penalty. Jesus and Paul never speak out against it, but their teachings set the Church on a collision course with this social practice (see Matthew 6:26; 10:24-31; Luke 15; also Galatians 3:28; Ephesians 6:5-9; Colossians 3:11; and others).

Hence Paul delicately deals with a sticky personal situation. Onesimus was a runaway slave. He possibly had stolen some money from his wealthy Christian master (Philemon 15, 18). Apparently by chance, he meets Paul in Rome and is converted to Christianity (verse 10). Paul, knowing it would be useful to keep Onesimus with him as a helper (verse 13), decides it best to return him to his owner, Philemon, with this brief letter. Philemon was a resident of Colossae in Phrygia and had been converted by Paul and had a Christian fellowship Church meeting at his home.

Summary of Contents

Paul opens his letter with a salutation and general thanksgiving. Then Paul pleads for Onesimus. Paul is "bold enough in Christ to command" Philemon concerning the status of Onesimus. But in Christian love, he pleads the case instead. He says he returns his heart with Onesimus, who is now more than a slave: he is a beloved brother. Paul requests that he receive Onesimus as he would receive Paul himself. Render no punishment. Charge any wrongs to Paul's account. He concludes by asking Philemon to prepare a guest room for him, for he hopes to be released and pay him a visit.

Some scholars believe that Onesimus was eventually returned to Paul and that this is the same Onesimus who became bishop of Ephesus (107-117), as mentioned by the Church Father Ignatius.

Passages for Everyday Living

I thank my God always when I remember you in my prayers. . . (Philemon 4).

The Christian faith is not to be lived in isolation. Paul is very appreciative of the need for fellowship, a fellowship that *reflects the center* of the faith, that is, fellowship with the Father through Christ and in the Holy Spirit. Paul always displays wonderful enthusiasm for Christian support, communion and acceptance. If Christianity is to be lived and taken seriously, it must be practiced in the fellowship of the saints.

* * *

> *Accordingly, though I am bold enough*
> *in Christ to command you to do what is re-*
> *quired, yet for love's sake I prefer to ap-*
> *peal to you — I, Paul, an ambassador and*
> *now a prisoner also for Christ Jesus — I*
> *appeal to you for my child, Onesimus,*
> *whose father I have become in my im-*
> *prisonment (Philemon 8-10).*

The brilliance of this letter lies in Paul's tact. He trusts not in his own political clout, but in the principle of love that had to have ruled Philemon's heart as a born-anew Christian brother. In other words, he relies upon God's grace. Onesimus had been converted and Paul was his spiritual father (1 Corinthians 4:15 and Galatians 4:19). "My child" is a strong term of affection and grace. Paul was so sure of his new child in the faith that he goes on to assure Philemon that Onesimus would now be "profitable" to him (Philemon 11).

Paul is practicing here what he had taught so many times before. Love is the ruling principle of the Christian's life, a love that reflects the love of God for humanity made known in Christ (see 1 Corinthians 13, for example). Paul now acts, *trusting* in that love, staking everything on its strength and power. Even his own apostolic authority cannot match the overwhelming influence of love. If Philemon was truly Christian, love would be the overriding value that would guide him in his dealing with Onesimus. As Jesus taught, how can one experience the forgiveness of God and not practice the same principle in dealings with fellow human beings? (See Jesus' parable, Matthew 18:21-35; Luke 7:41-43; Matthew 7:12, 14-15.)

* * *

> *Perhaps this is why he was parted*

from you for a while, that you might have
him back for ever, no longer as a slave but
more than a slave, as a beloved brother,
especially to me but how much more to
you, both in the flesh and in the Lord
(Philemon 15-16).

Paul does not miss the opportunity to comment on God's providence. God provides a way for people to hear His message and learn of His love. They may reject His plan and His grace, but they will hear, if only through the silence of a starry night, the beauty of a sunset, the wonderful music of a Mozart concerto or by way of some unusual circumstances. Now, through the grace of God, Onesimus returns much more than just an individual. He is of the highest value, a fellow believer in Christ.

Paul concludes with words that leave no doubt about his expectations: "Yes, brother, I want some benefit from you in the Lord. Refresh my heart in Christ. Confident of your obedience, I write to you, knowing that you will do even more than I say" (Philemon 20-21).

Index

distress — 73

emotions — 97f
encouragement — 79f, 161, 178f
end time — 94, 183, 185, 188
Eucharist — 84, 94
evil — 188
example (Christ's) — 148
experience — 59f, 84, 89f, 97f, 117, 158f, 179f, 184

fainthearted — 186
faith — 57, 60, 84, 88f, 92, 105f, 114f, 120, 124f, 126, 131, 135f, 141, 145,
   148, 153f, 162, 167, 177, 179, 187, 189f, 193
family — 75, 173
Father — 68, 123, 138, 162f
fear — 153
fellowship — 109, 120, 126f, 150, 154f, 161, 163f, 167, 170f, 184f, 187, 192
forgiveness — 64, 172
Francis of Assisi — 128
freedom — 58f, 65f, 139, 154
fruits of the Spirit — 123
future — 26f

Gamaliel — 32
Gentile Christians — 54f, 111f
gifts (spiritual) — 72, 84, 97, 108, 137, 141, 144, 147
glory of God — 62, 95, 104, 120
goals — 69
God's purpose — 71f, 74
God's will — 134
Gospel — 35, 58f, 61, 88f, 100f, 106, 133, 147
grace — 12, 62, 87f, 104, 107f, 112, 114, 116, 132, 141, 144, 152, 154, 180f
Greeks — 89, 125
growing (in faith) — 66, 92, 142, 162, 168

healing — 97, 100, 124
Hellenism — 18, 30, 36
holiness — 75
Holy Spirit — 19, 47, 50ff, 67, 72, 77, 84, 90ff, 97, 102, 108f, 110f, 123ff,
   128, 138f, 140, 143, 145, 152, 156, 172, 176, 178, 182f, 188
hope — 171, 180
husband — 144f
hymn — 151

James — 37, 43
Jewish — 29f, 38f, 53ff, 75, 89f, 93, 104, 111f, 121, 149, 159, 183, 189
joy — 124, 165
Judaizers — 38, 113ff, 130f, 158f
justification — 59

kingdom of God — 93
knowledge — 88, 171

law — 38f, 42f, 54f, 122, 124f

197